Road Noise

Marine

Memory Exercise

Holly Myers

then/and

then/and publications
ISBN 978-1-947322-92-9

Road Noise

Rocks like bleached bones, huge and prehistoric.
Flowers in waves of color across the grass.

It was a relief when the land let loose around the river.

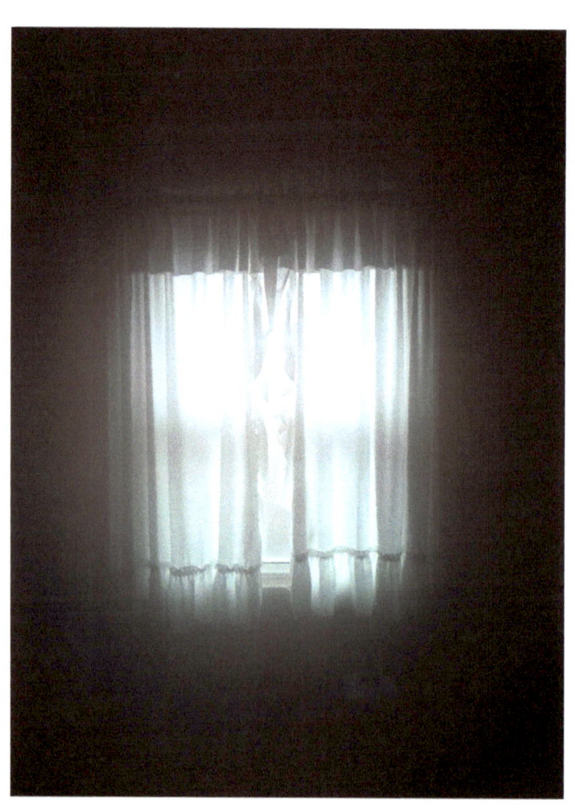

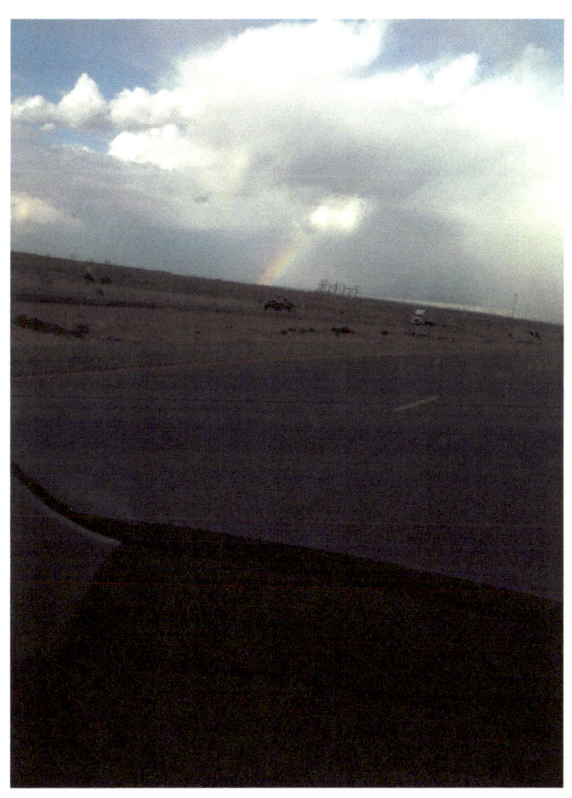

A million of these.

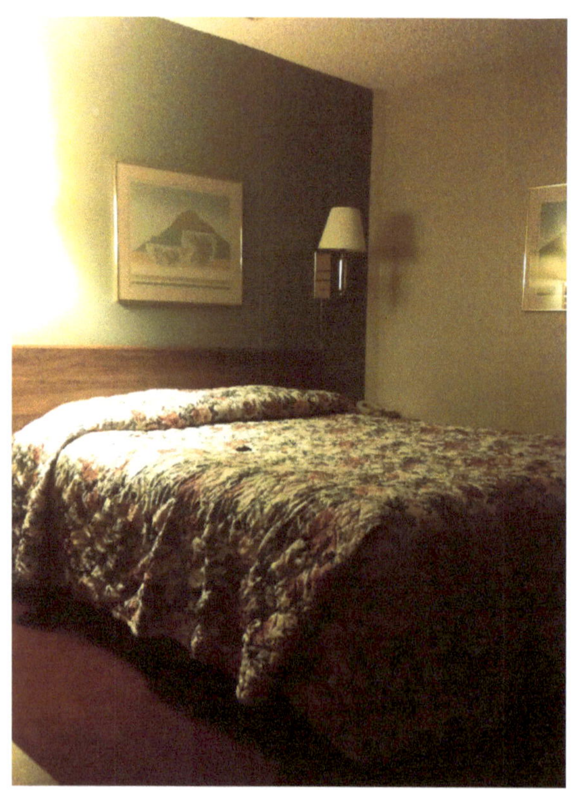

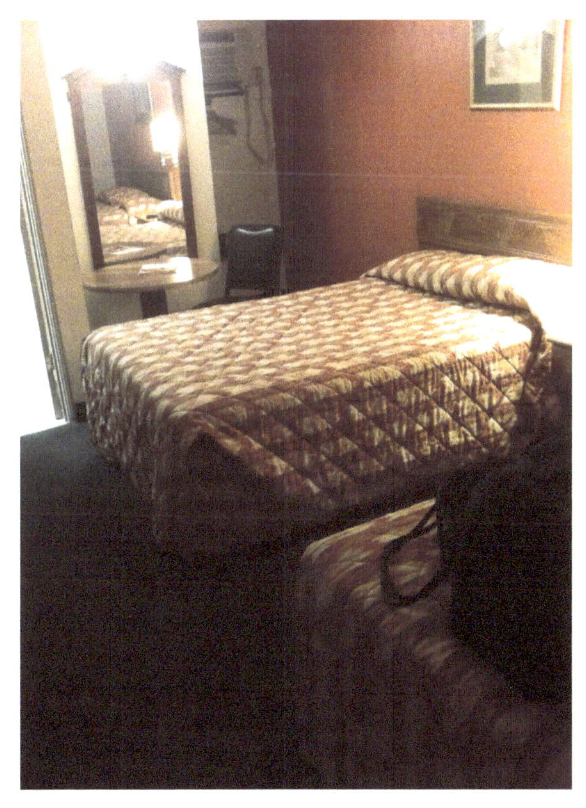

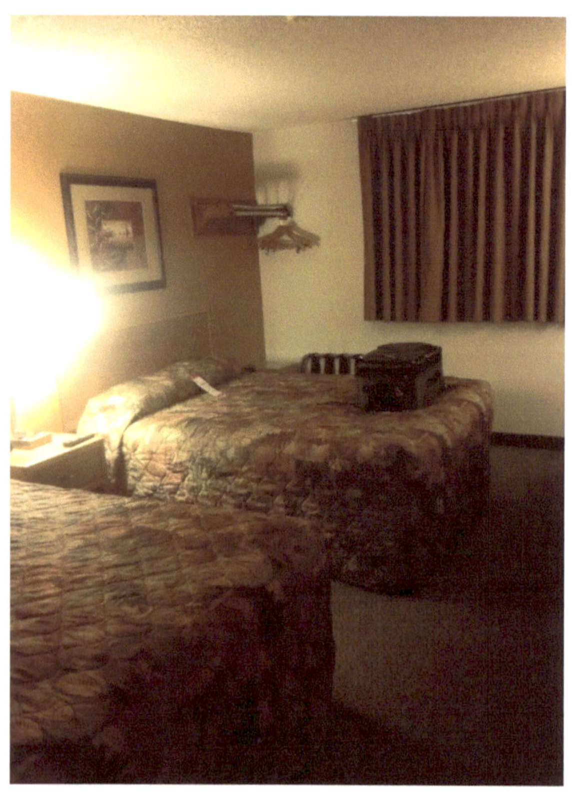

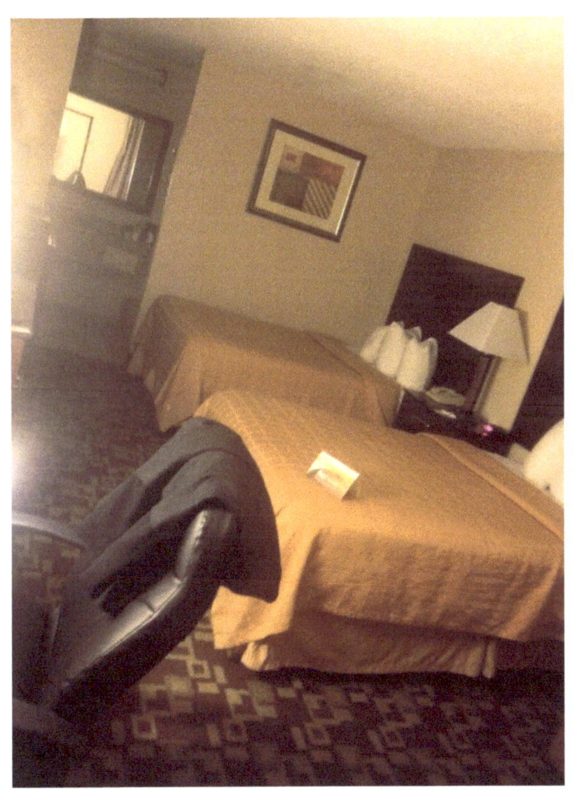

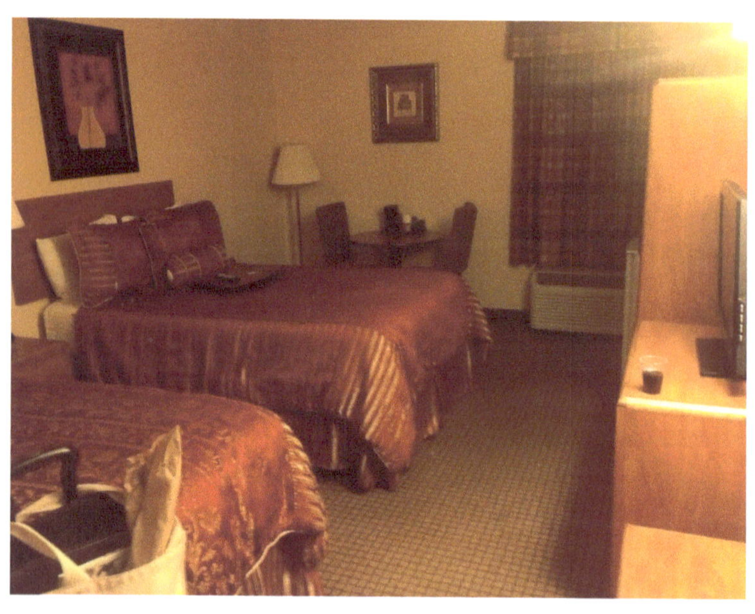

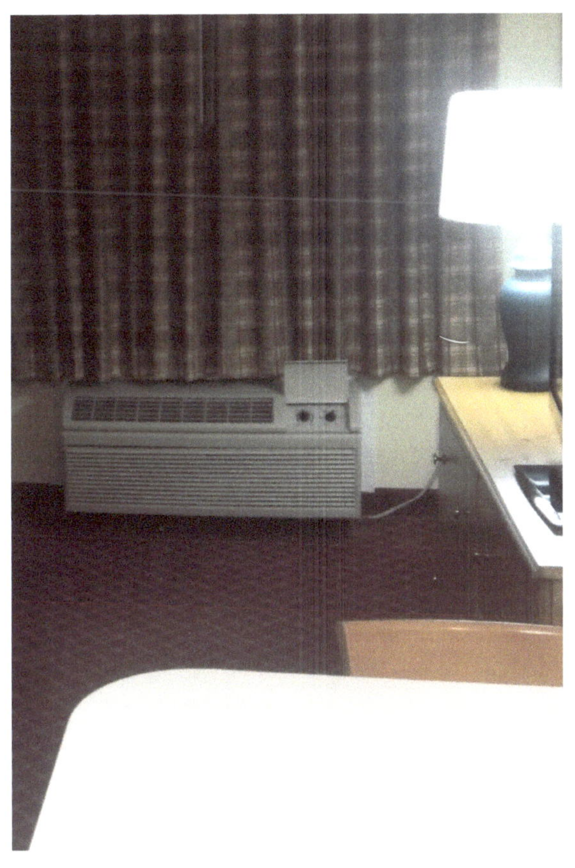

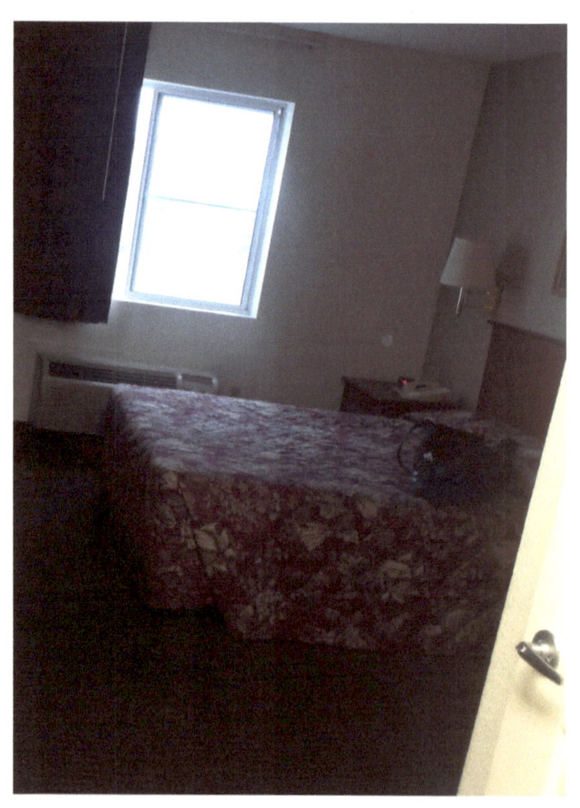

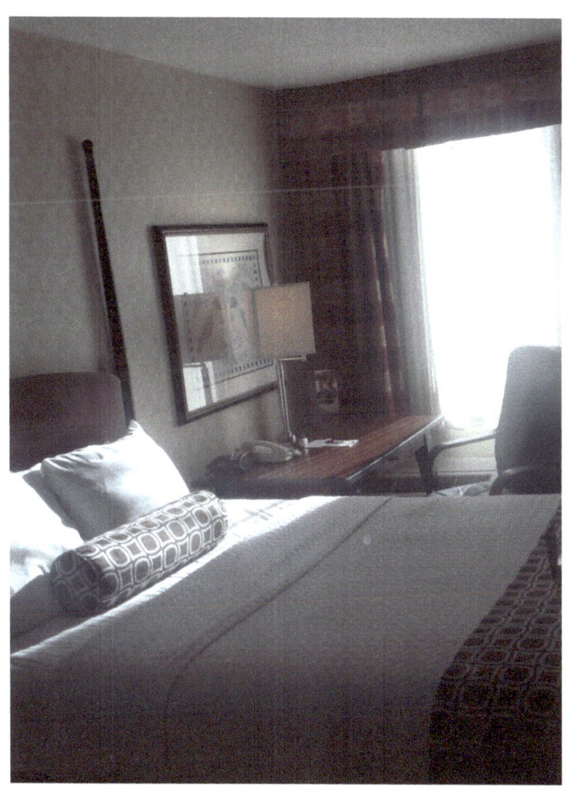

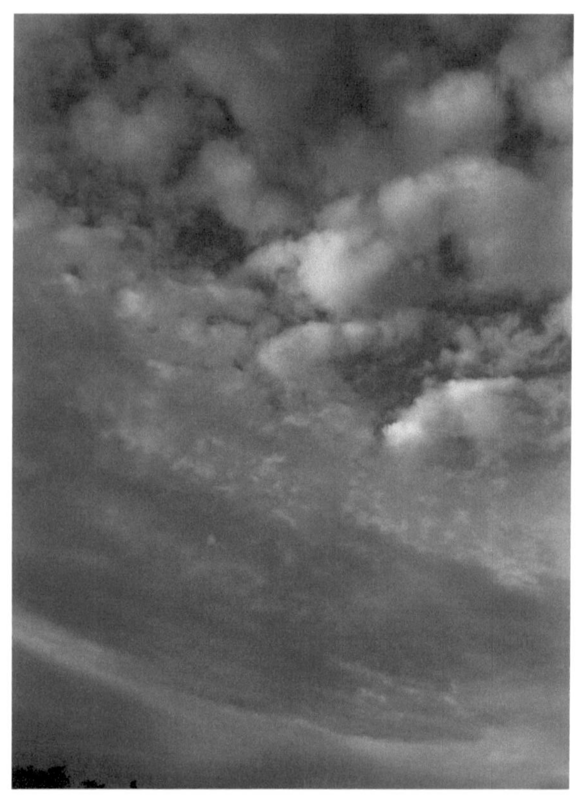

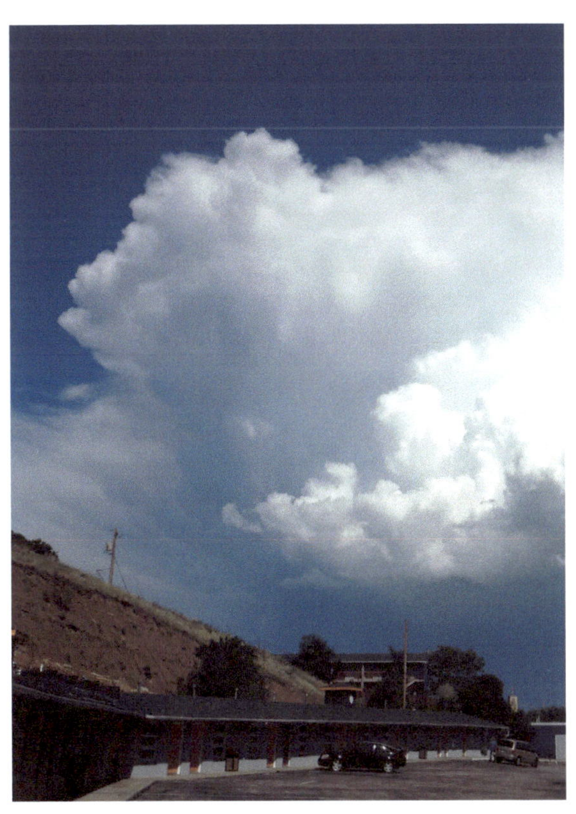

Sleeping, highway noises.

The sunlight slid across the surface of the wild
yellow grass.
The wild space, the sky.
There was a storefront for rent in a small town.

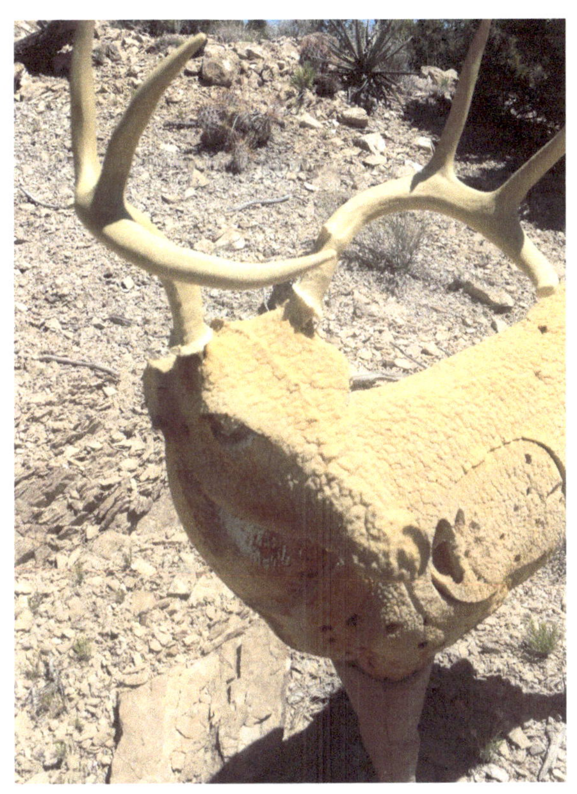

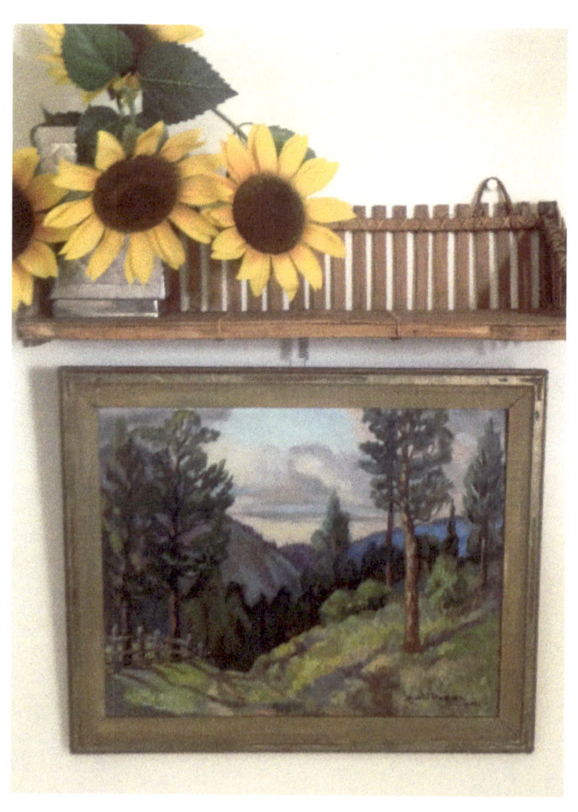

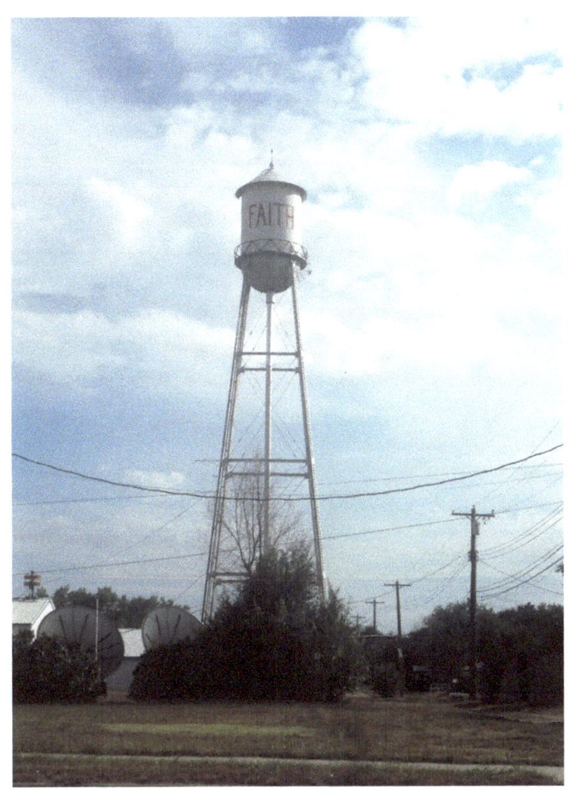
FAITH

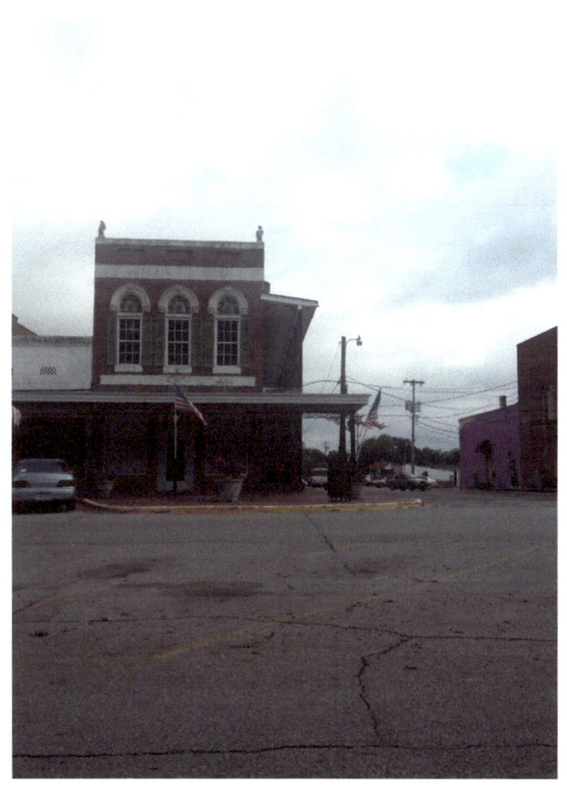

Aquarius (Jan. 20-Feb. 18): Tasks that would usually be rote seem to have a different meaning now. You're heading for a breakthrough.

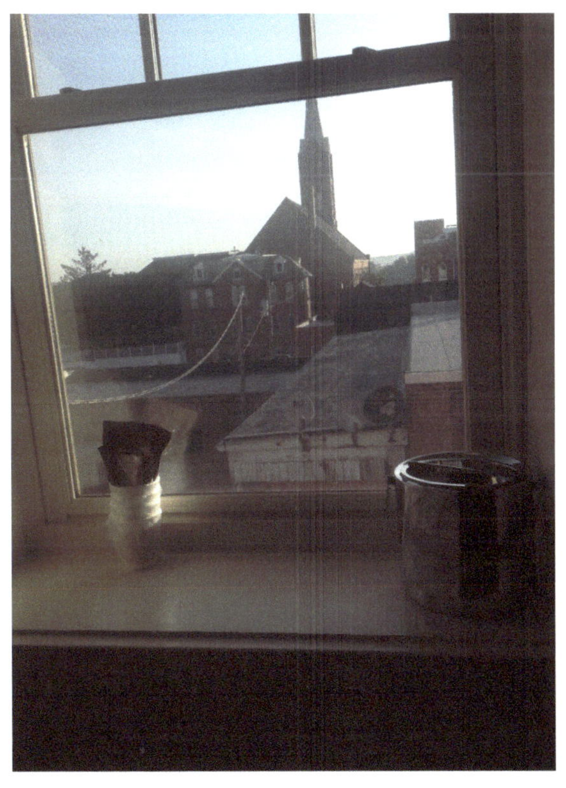

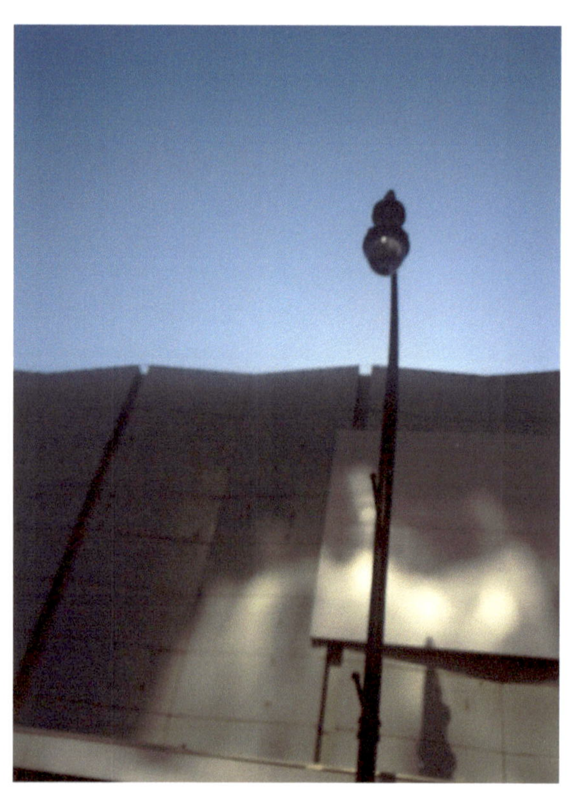

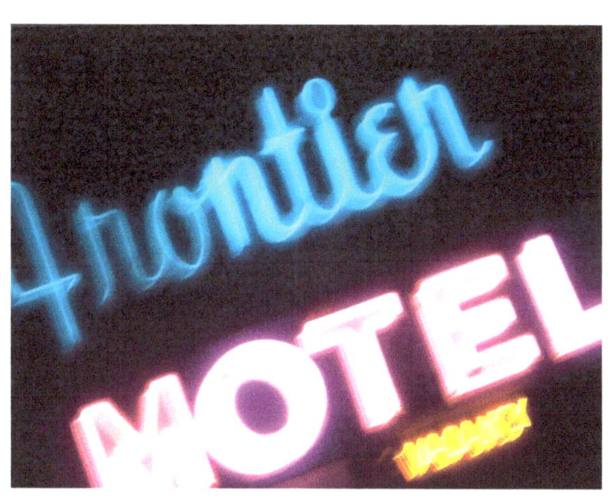
Frontier
MOTEL

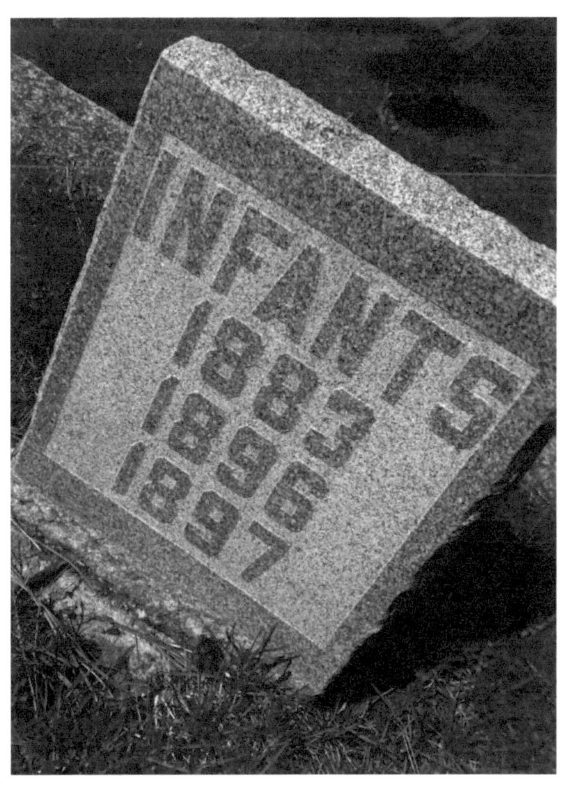
INFANTS
1883
1896
1897

A strange collision of close and remote.
The ruins of a church.
The ruins of a schoolhouse.

There is no silence.
Insects, cattle, wind, soil.

A motorcycle alone in a field.

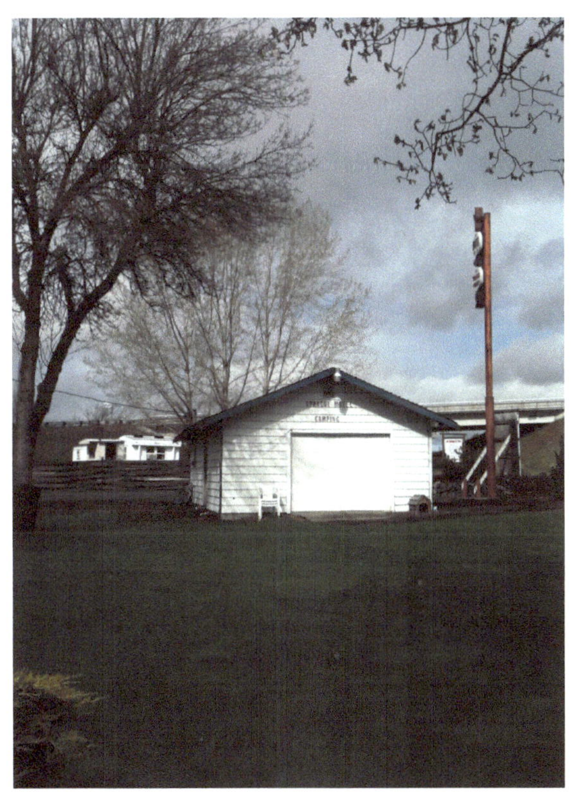
CAMPING

There was a man in a bar called the Blue Rooster
who said he had taught himself how to read Latin.
There was another man recently out of prison.
Still there were tales of Spanish gold, apparently, and
the bar was just about all that was open there.

A shabby street,
hollowed out in every meaningful crevice.

The hum of a small refrigerator.

All across America.

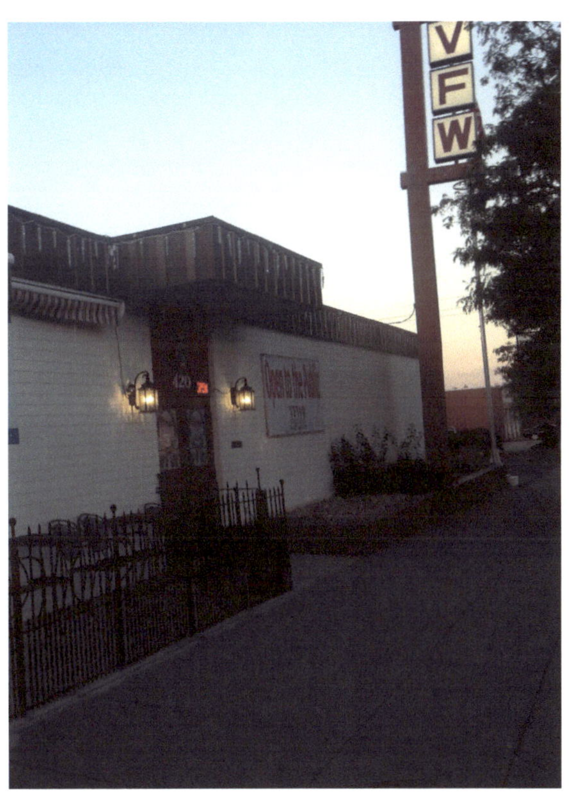
VFW
420

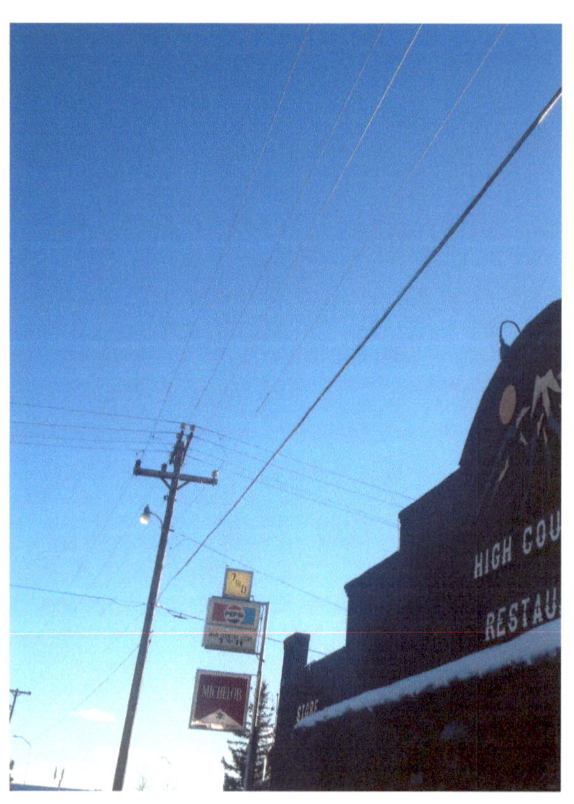
PEPSI
MICHELOB
HIGH COU
RESTAU

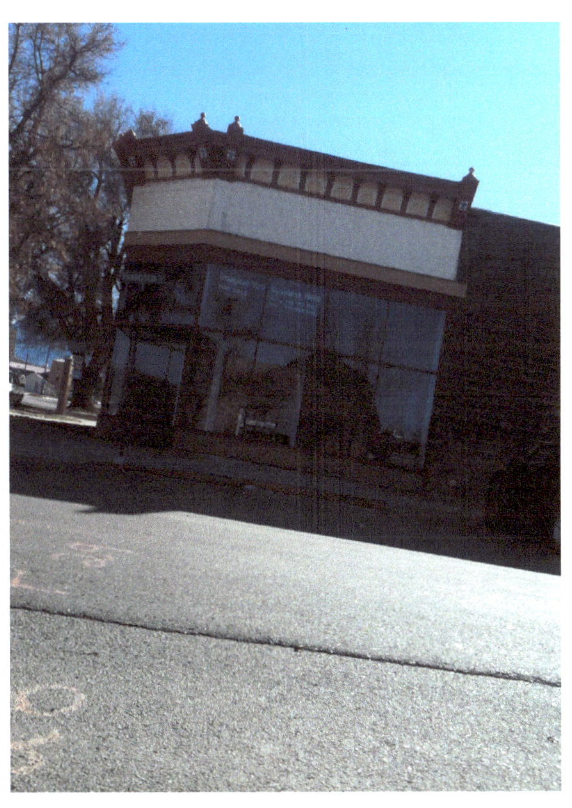

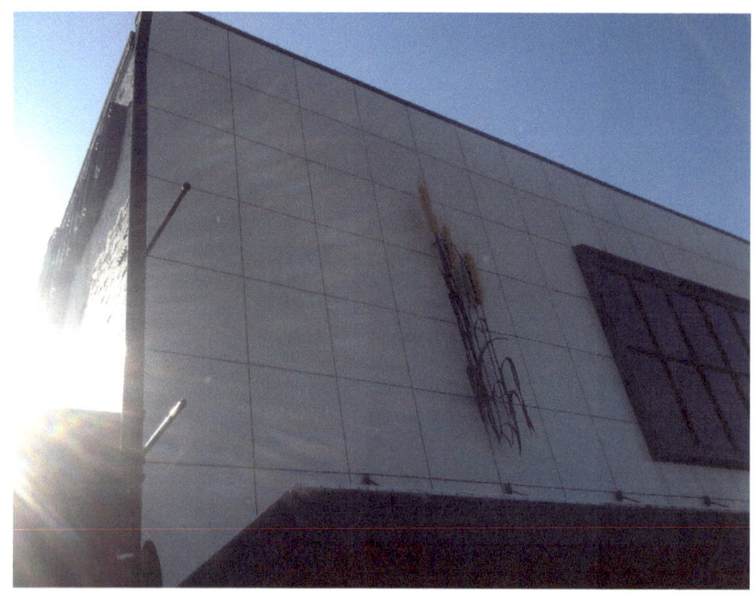

Solitary windmills.
There were oil derricks.
Semi trucks, oil trucks, pick up trucks,
men of a hard kind, untempered.

A swarming of trucks. The place south of there
was very old; a pit full of bones,
fantastic creatures.

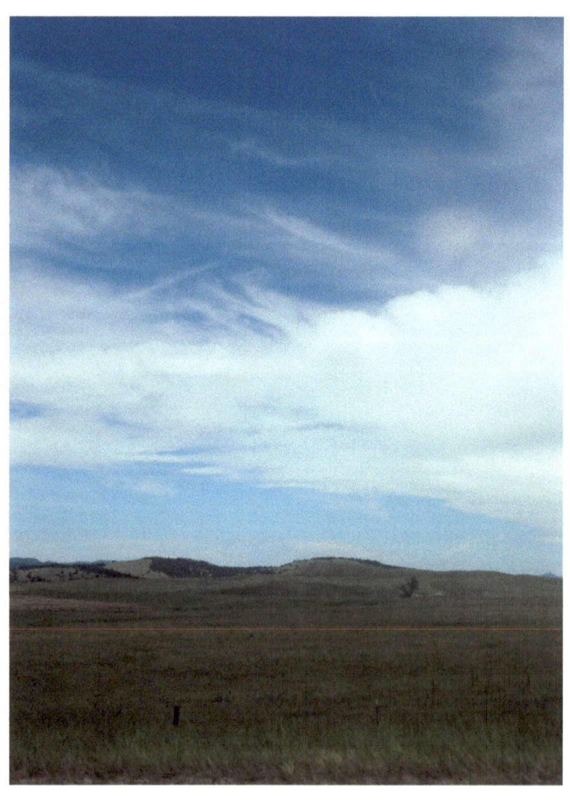

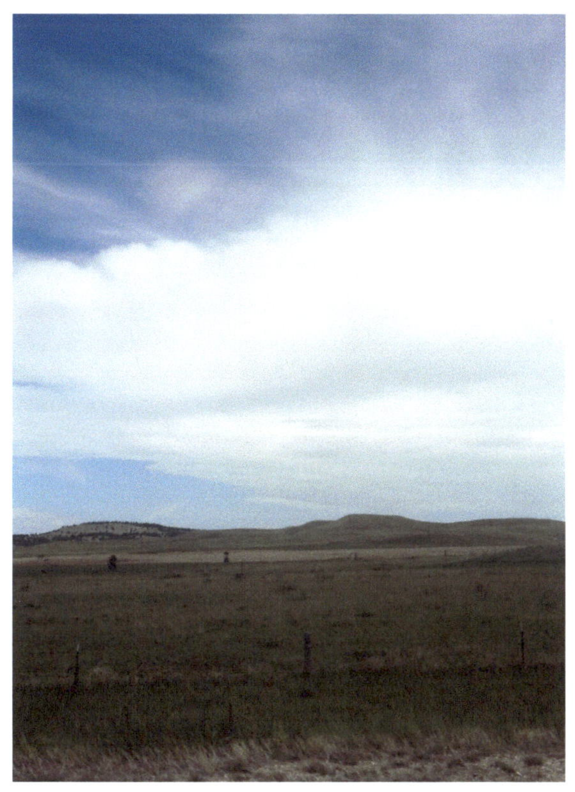

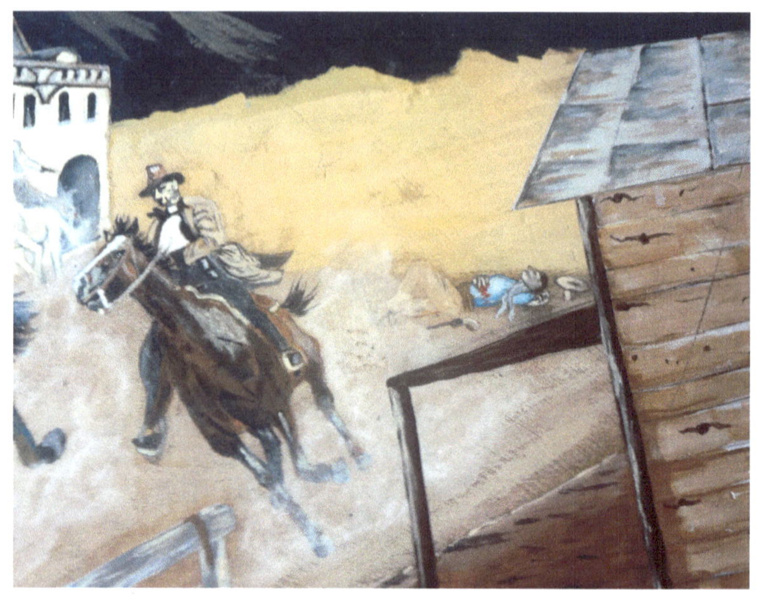

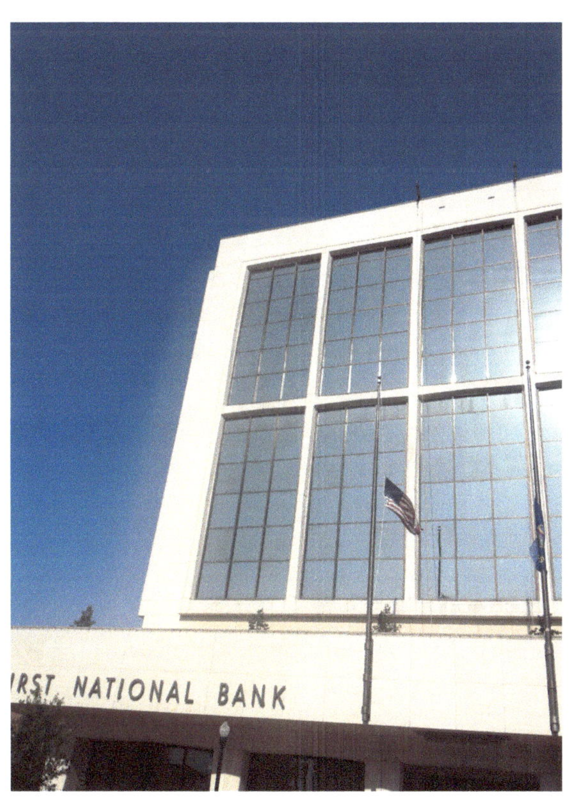
RST NATIONAL BANK

Golden light on a white plank fence.

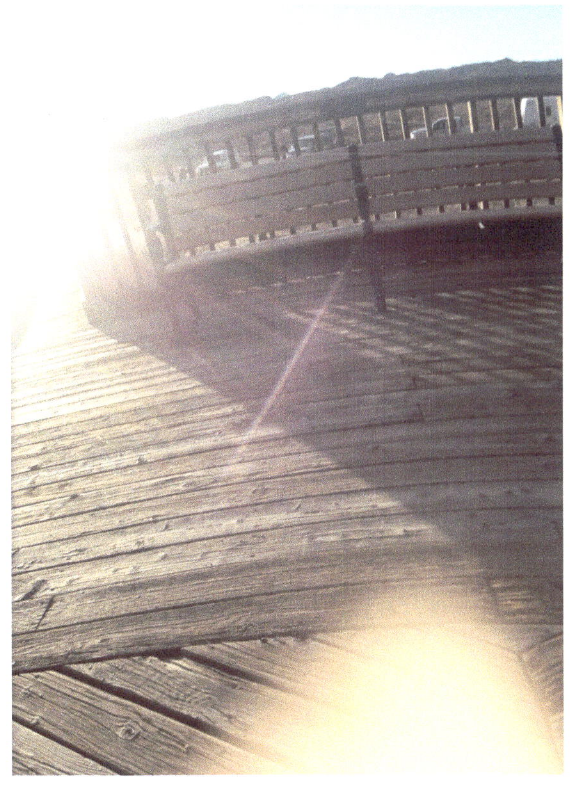

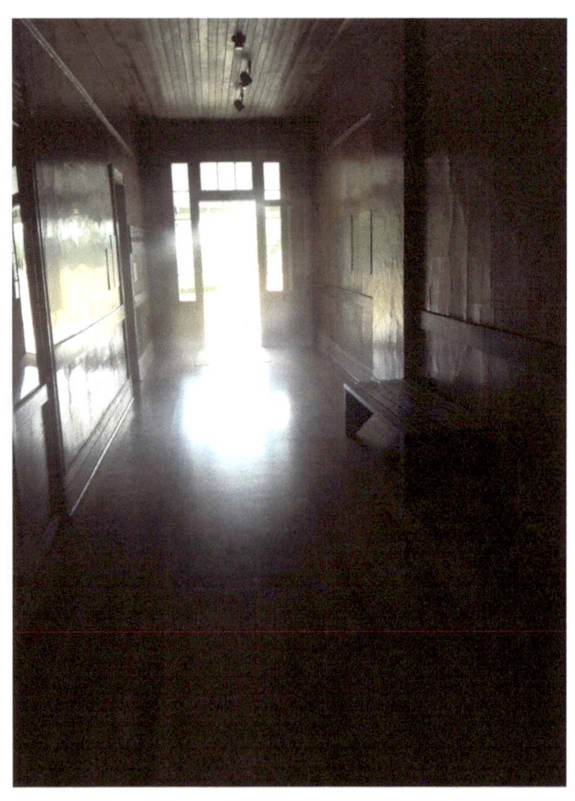

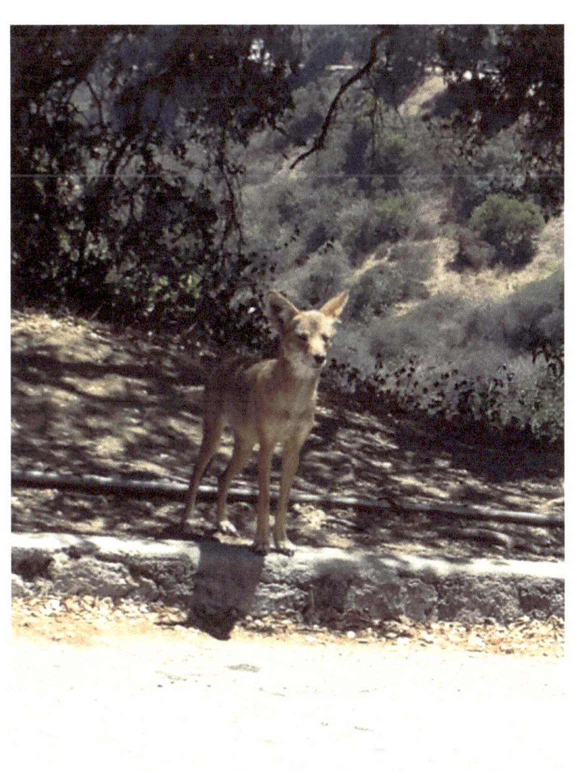

You're headed for a breakthrough.

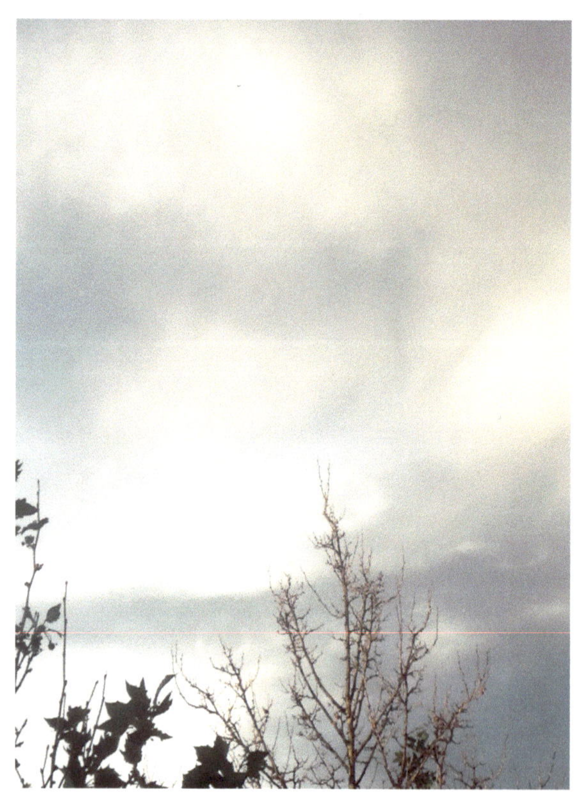

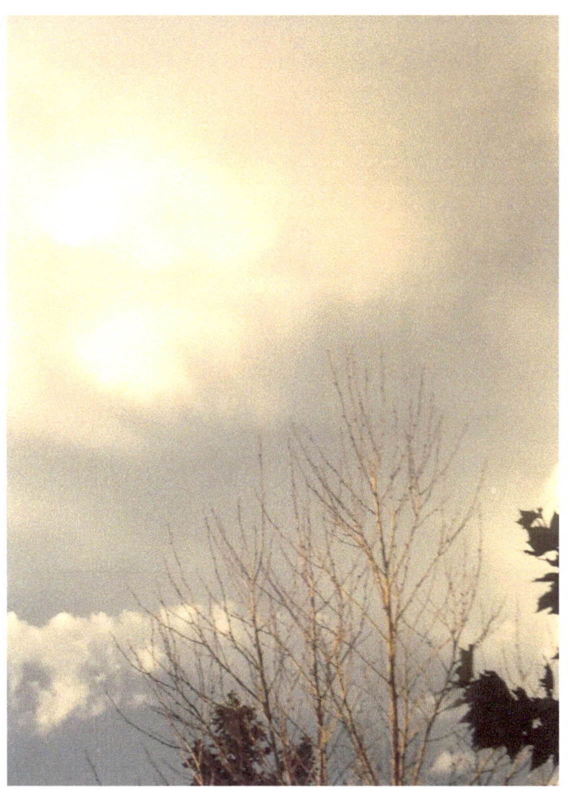

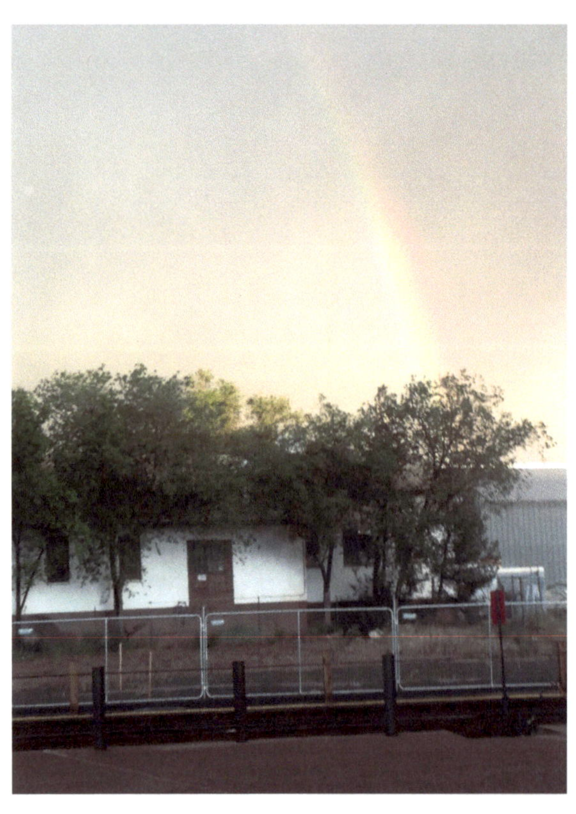

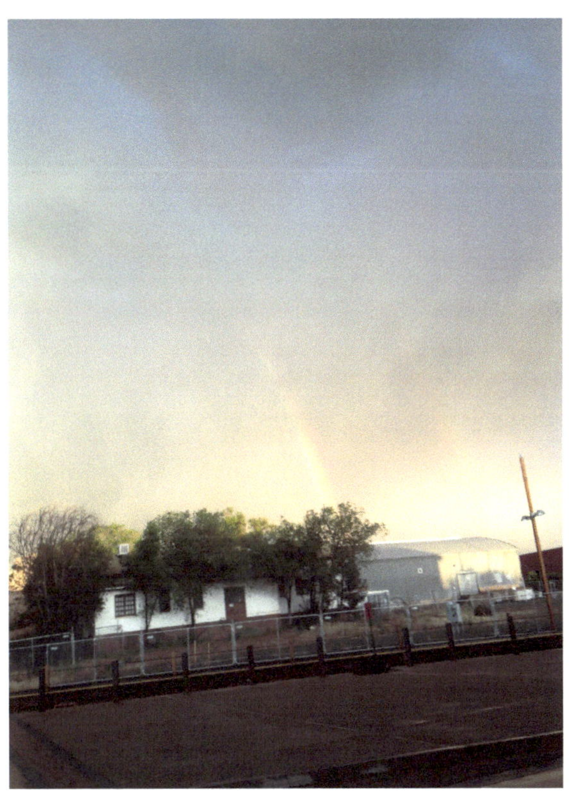

Marine

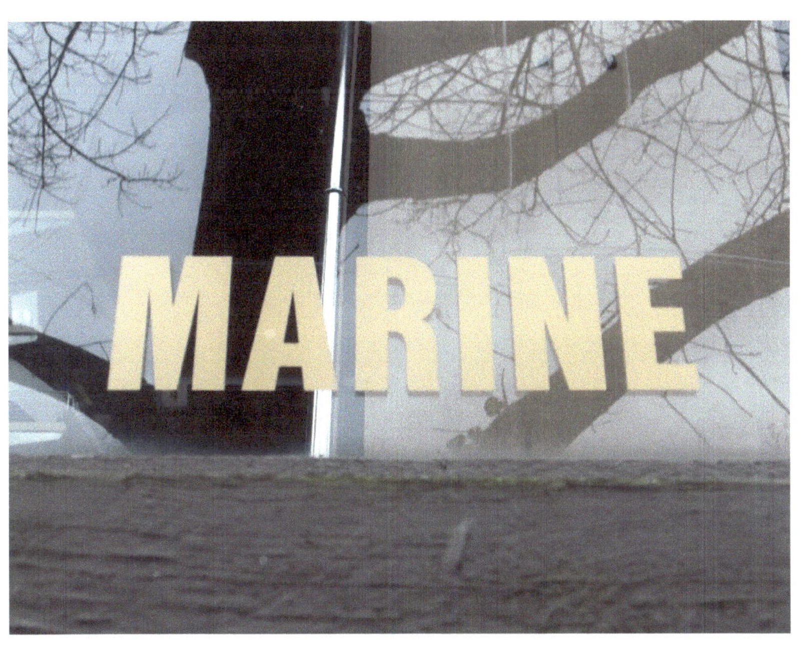
MARINE

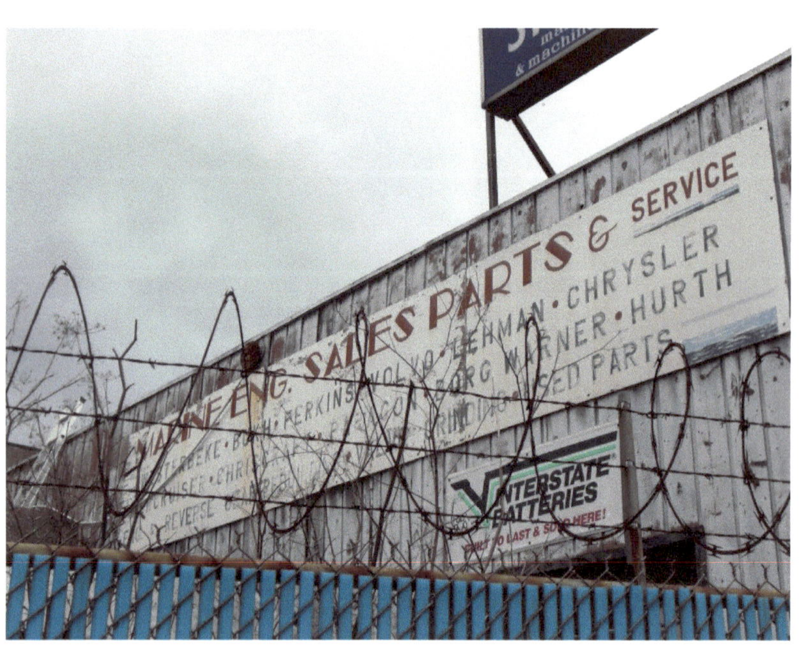
MARINE ENG. SALES PARTS & SERVICE
LEHMAN • CHRYSLER
BORG WARNER • HURTH
PERKINS
INTERSTATE BATTERIES

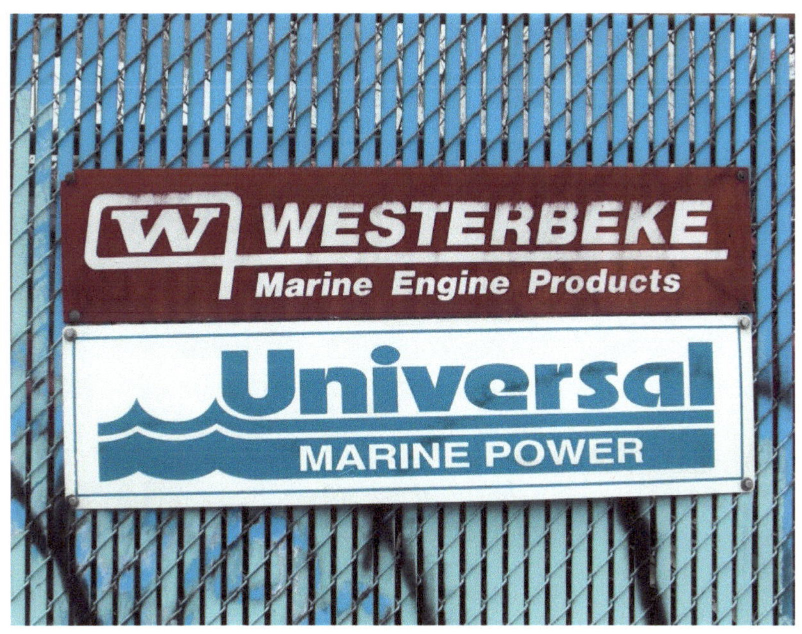
W
WESTERBEKE
Marine Engine Products
Universal
MARINE POWER

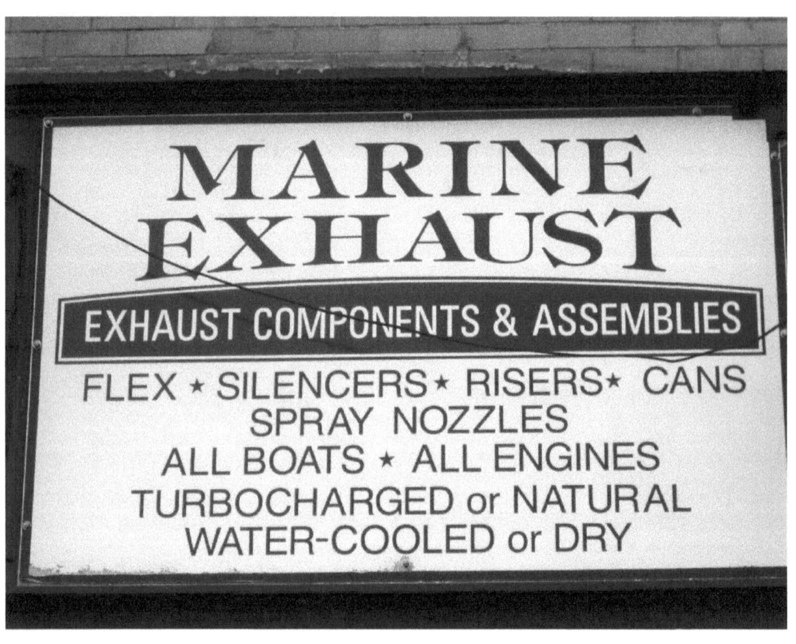
MARINE
EXHAUST
EXHAUST COMPONENTS & ASSEMBLIES
FLEX ★ SILENCERS ★ RISERS ★ CANS
SPRAY NOZZLES
ALL BOATS ★ ALL ENGINES
TURBOCHARGED or NATURAL
WATER-COOLED or DRY

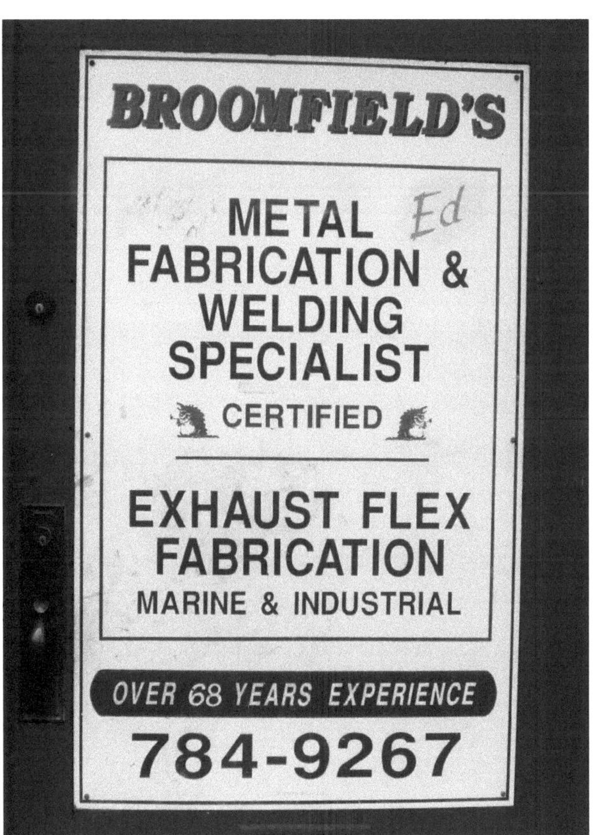
BROOMFIELD'S
METAL
Ed
FABRICATION &
WELDING
SPECIALIST
CERTIFIED
EXHAUST FLEX
FABRICATION
MARINE & INDUSTRIAL
OVER 68 YEARS EXPERIENCE
784-9267

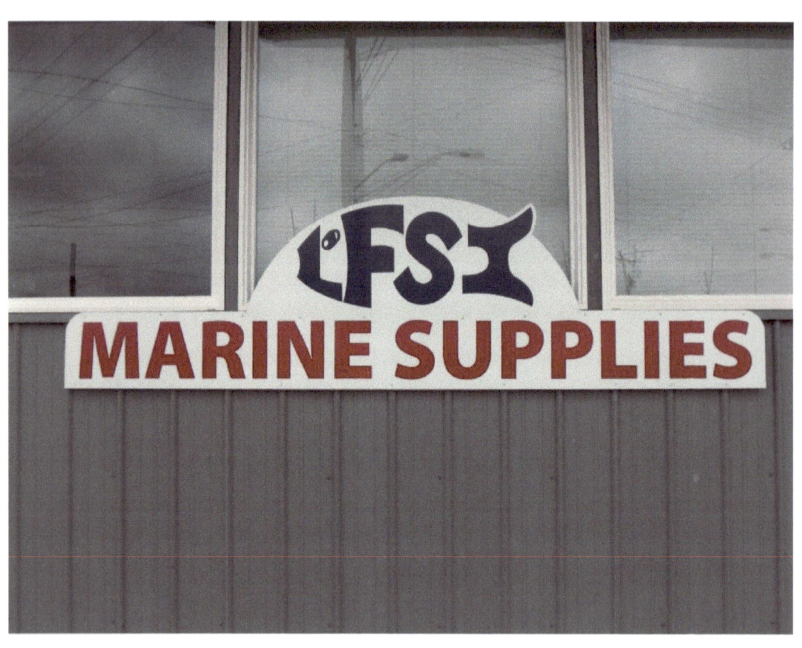
LFSI
MARINE SUPPLIES

SCANDINAVIAN
FISHING EQUIPMENT

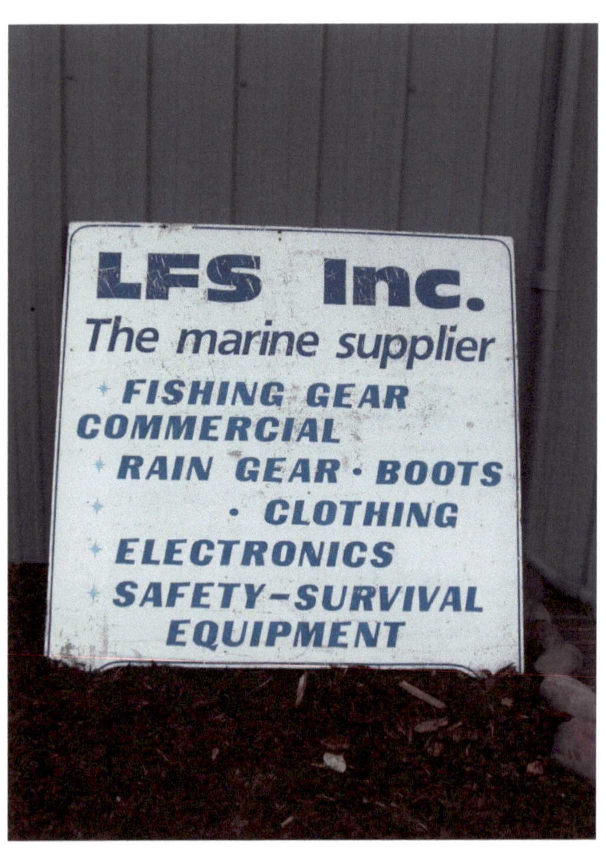
LFS Inc.
The marine supplier
FISHING GEAR
COMMERCIAL
RAIN GEAR · BOOTS
· CLOTHING
ELECTRONICS
SAFETY–SURVIVAL
EQUIPMENT

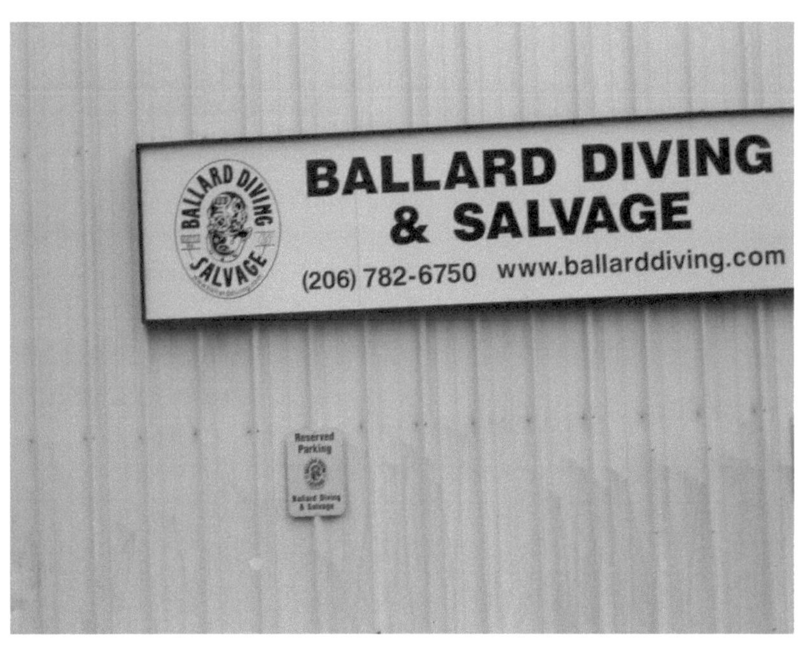
BALLARD DIVING
& SALVAGE
(206) 782-6750 www.ballarddiving.com
BALLARD DIVING
SALVAGE

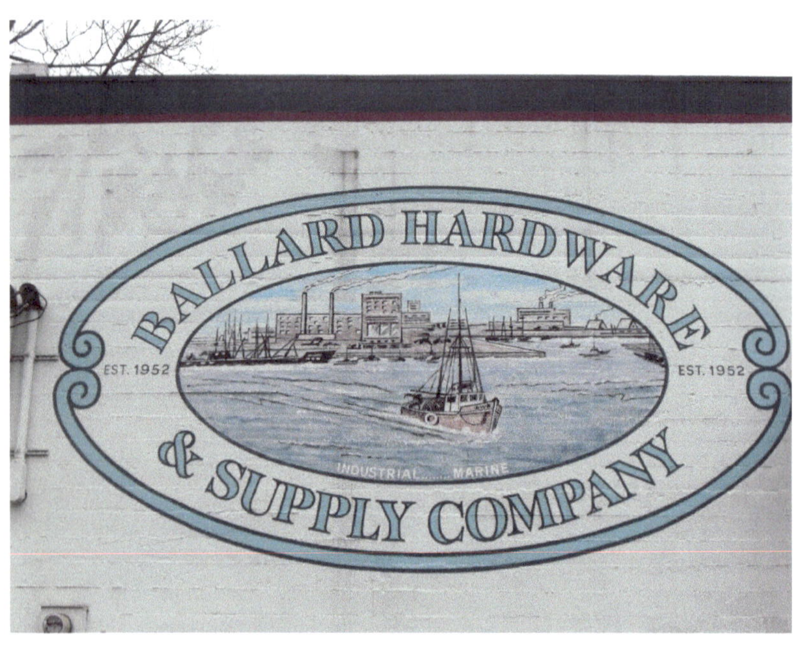
BALLARD HARDWARE
EST. 1952
EST. 1952
INDUSTRIAL...... MARINE
& SUPPLY COMPANY

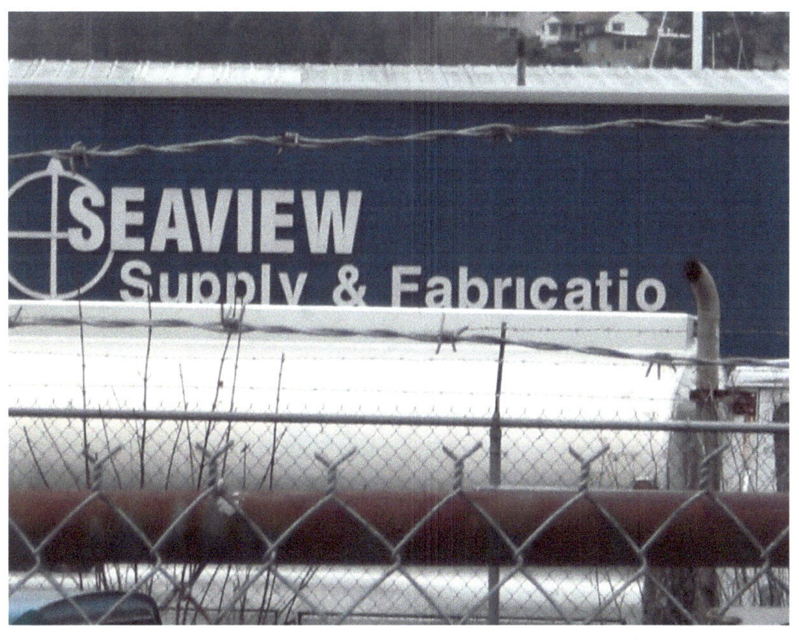
SEAVIEW
Supply & Fabricatio

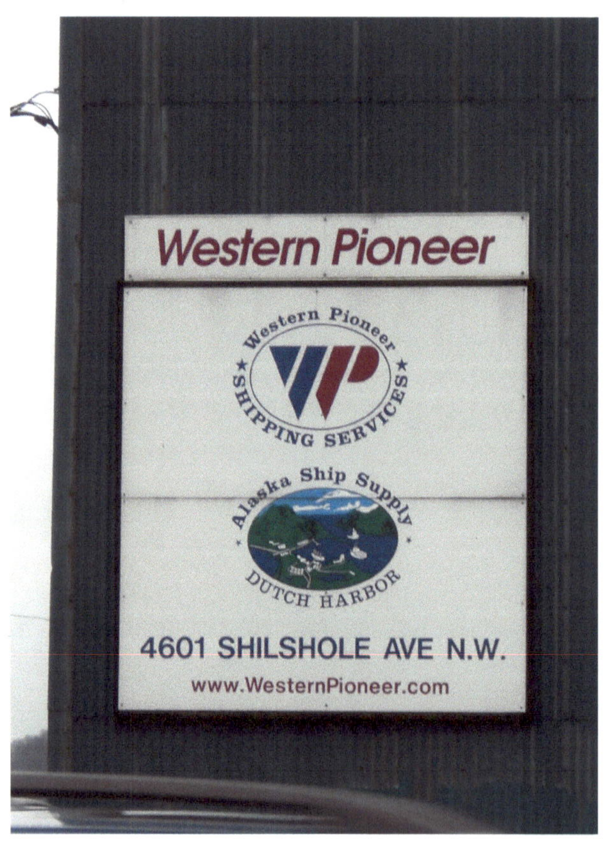
Western Pioneer
Western Pioneer
SHIPPING SERVICES
Alaska Ship Supply
DUTCH HARBOR
4601 SHILSHOLE AVE N.W.
www.WesternPioneer.com

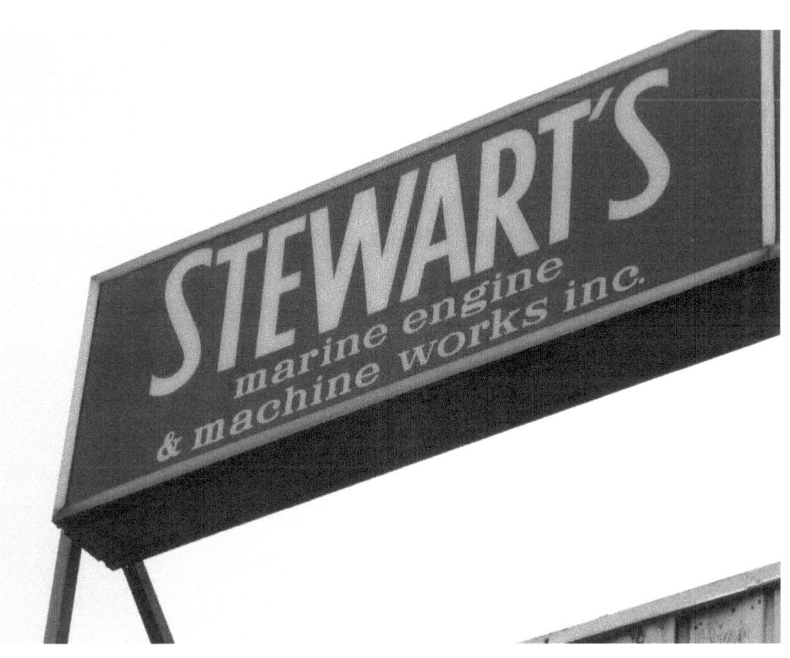
STEWART'S
marine engine
& machine works inc.

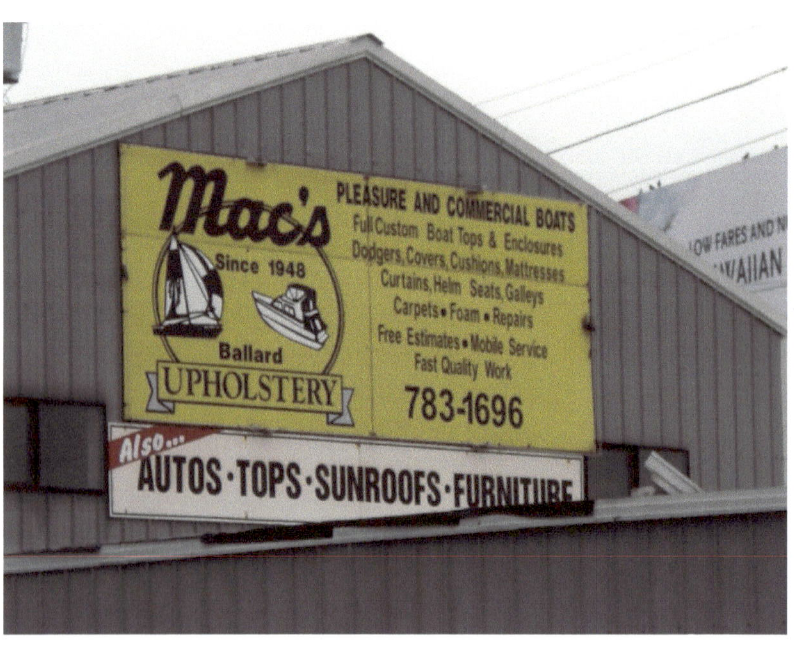
Mac's
Since 1948
Ballard
UPHOLSTERY
PLEASURE AND COMMERCIAL BOATS
Full Custom Boat Tops & Enclosures
Dodgers, Covers, Cushions, Mattresses
Curtains, Helm Seats, Galleys
Carpets • Foam • Repairs
Free Estimates • Mobile Service
Fast Quality Work
783-1696
Also...
AUTOS · TOPS · SUNROOFS · FURNITURE

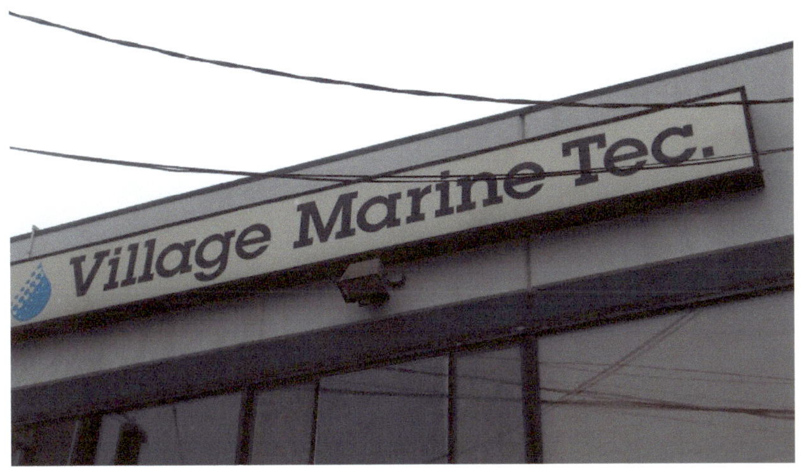
Village Marine Tec.

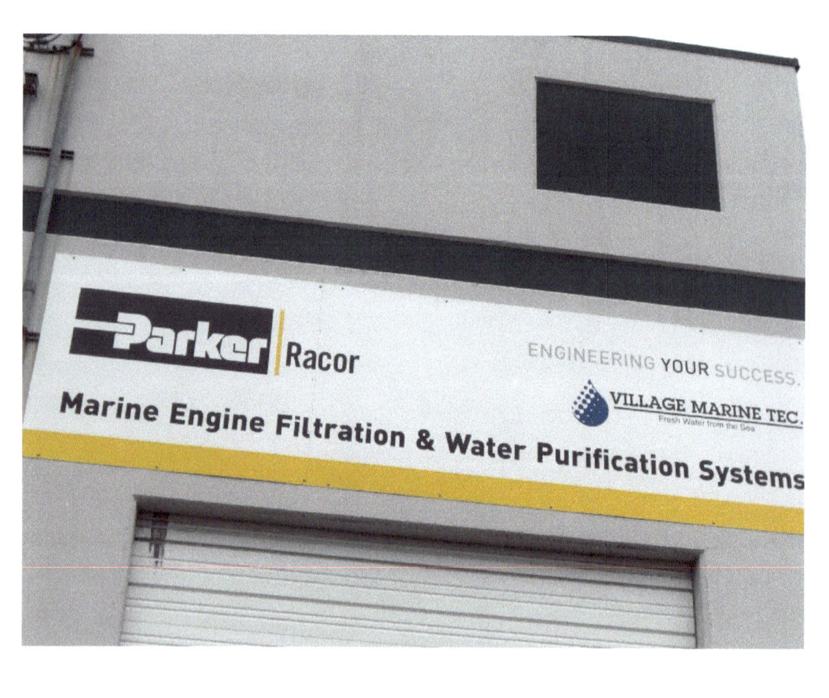
Parker
Racor
ENGINEERING YOUR SUCCESS.
VILLAGE MARINE TEC.
Marine Engine Filtration & Water Purification Systems

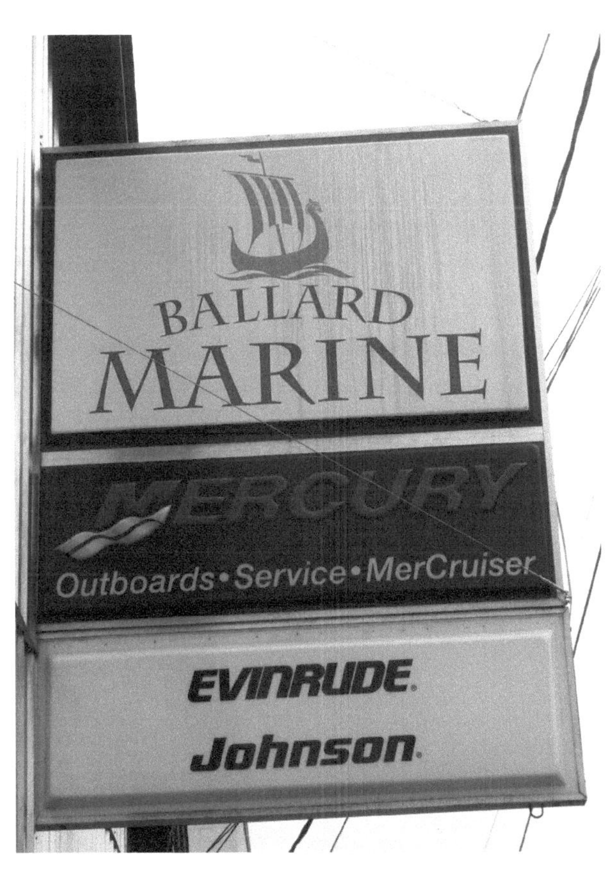
BALLARD
MARINE
MERCURY
Outboards • Service • MerCruiser
EVINRUDE.
Johnson.

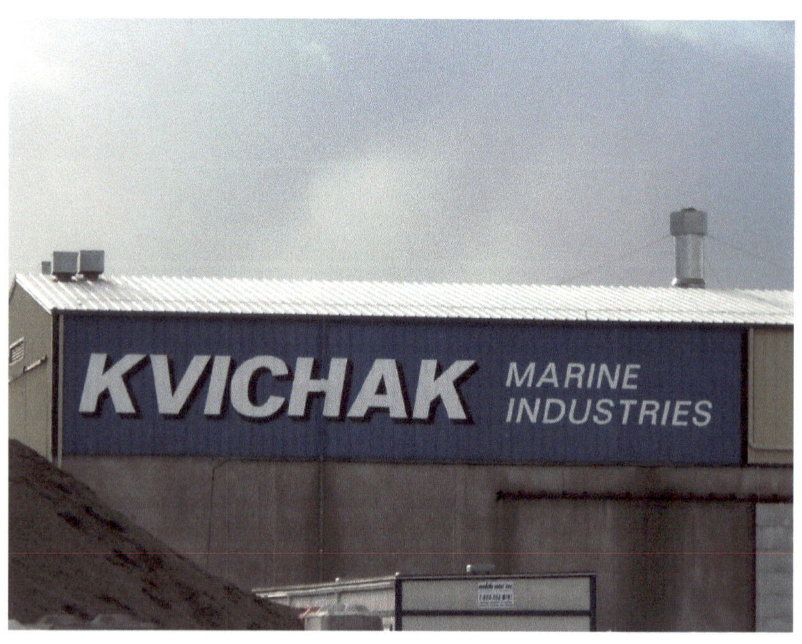
KVICHAK
MARINE
INDUSTRIES

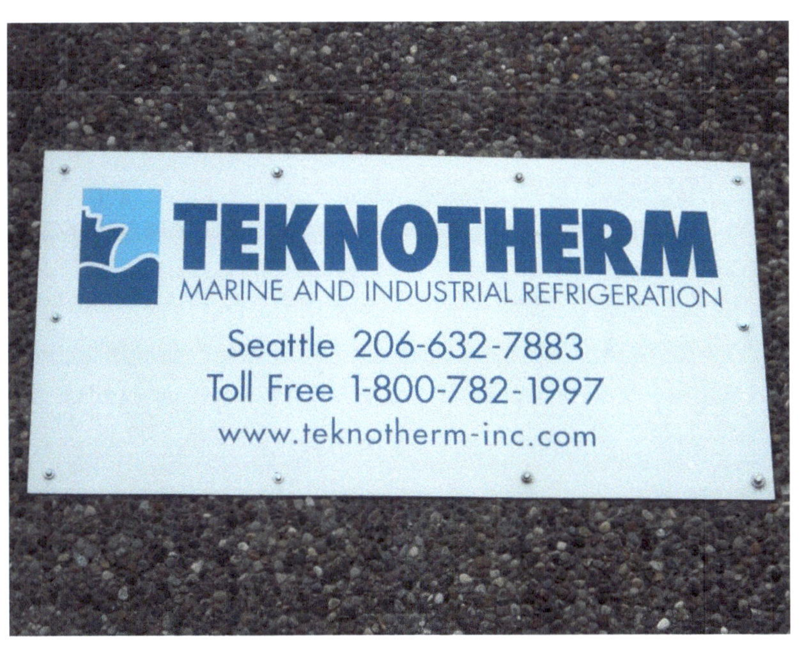
TEKNOTHERM
MARINE AND INDUSTRIAL REFRIGERATION
Seattle 206-632-7883
Toll Free 1-800-782-1997
www.teknotherm-inc.com

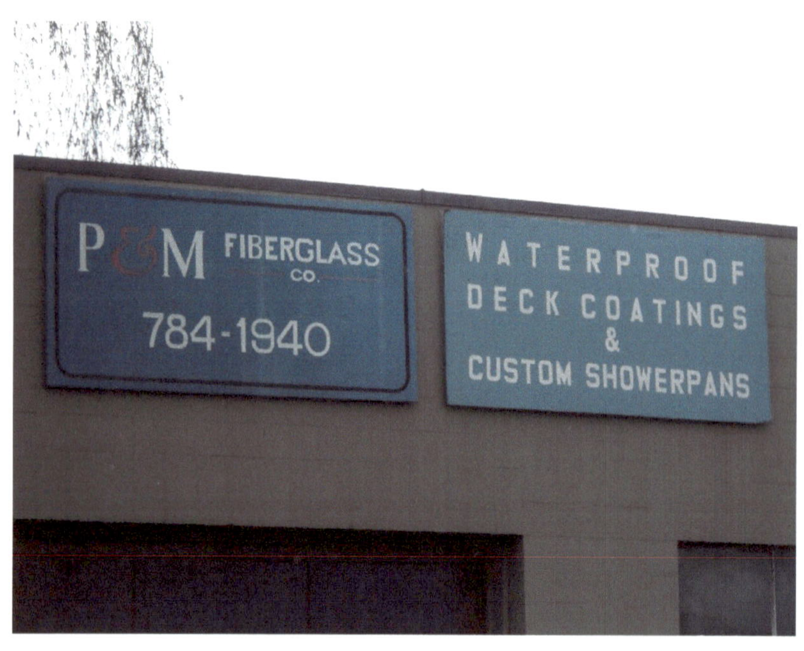
P&M FIBERGLASS CO.
784-1940
WATERPROOF
DECK COATINGS
&
CUSTOM SHOWERPANS

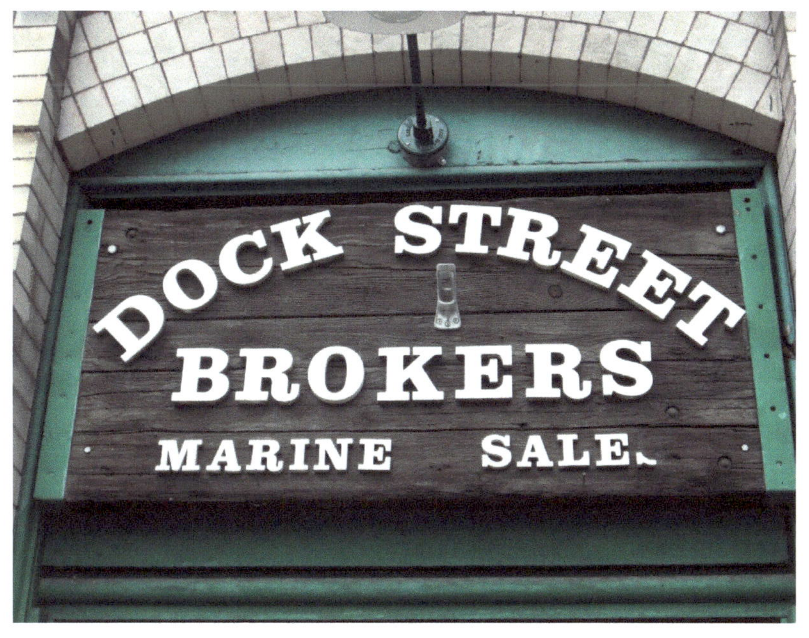
DOCK STREET
BROKERS
MARINE SALE

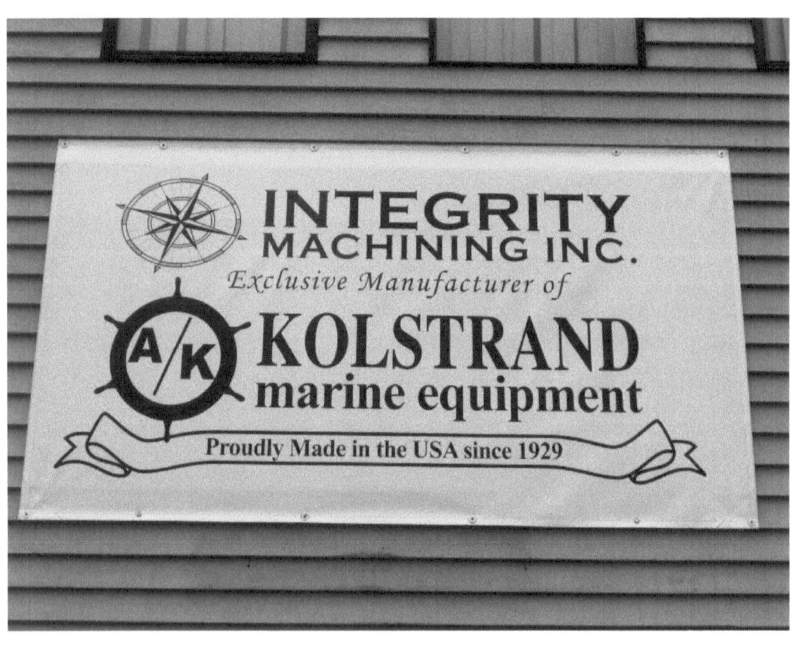
INTEGRITY
MACHINING INC.
Exclusive Manufacturer of
A/K
KOLSTRAND
marine equipment
Proudly Made in the USA since 1929

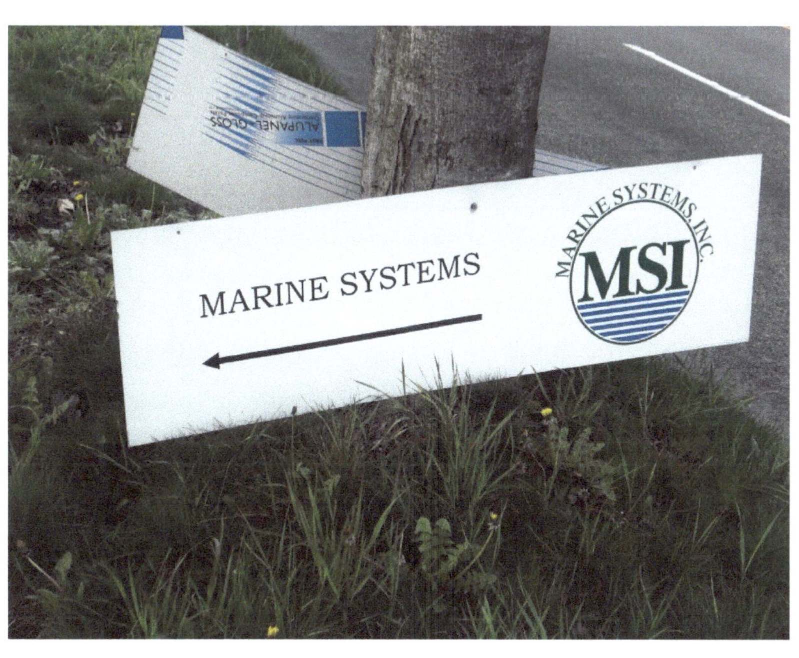
MARINE SYSTEMS
MARINE SYSTEMS, INC.
MSI

All deep, earnest thinking is but the intrepid effort of the soul to keep the open independence of her sea; while the wildest winds of heaven and earth conspire to cast her on the treacherous, slavish shore.

Herman Melville

Memory Exercise

I have been to Deadwood.
I have seen the grave of Calamity Jane.

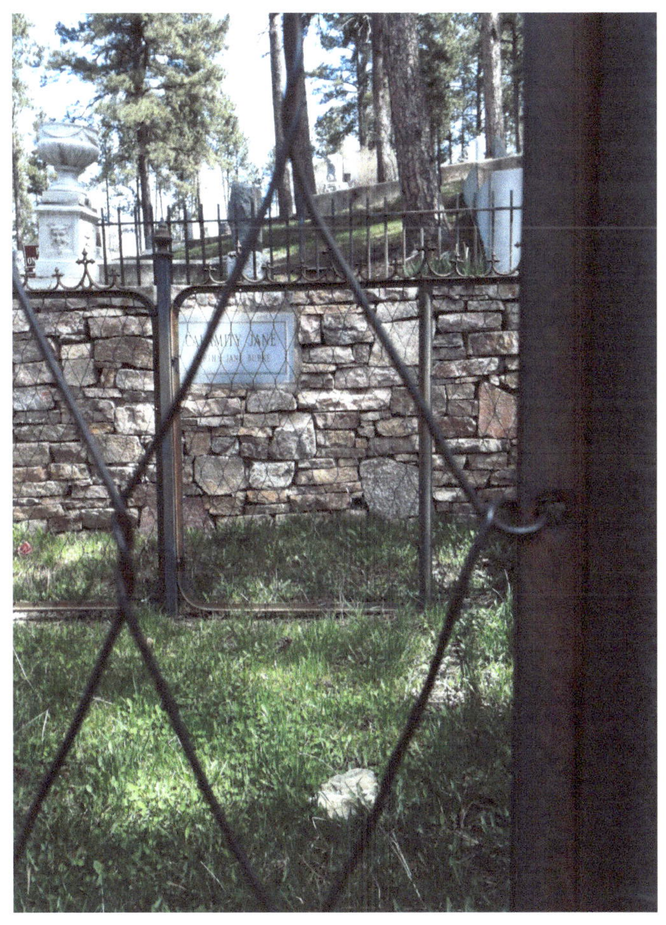

Blood on the Tracks is a long ribbon road in the vicinity of Galisteo, New Mexico. It is a feeling of late adolescence to start. It is a feeling of travel. The car changed everything. There was a summer we went to a spring somewhere, a pool in the ground, in the afternoon. There was a summer we wandered beneath the full blue moon through narrow, striated sandstone passages with a Danish boy no one ever saw again. That was Portishead, then, and an untroubled climate. But it wasn't all like that; the we there was actually precarious and slight. The car was a place of privacy, eloquence and power.

Blue is a New England college town. You said you were not much to speak of so far as fireworks went but clearly something stuck, a certain affinity. I remember late nights across inadvisable terrain. I admired, perhaps, the vigor of your intellect. I remember ice in the winter across the sidewalks and walls and a green spring and in that last spring a certain feeling of comfort.

Blood Sugar Sex Magic is an interstate, long and straight, east-west. But By the Way is a winding mountain road.

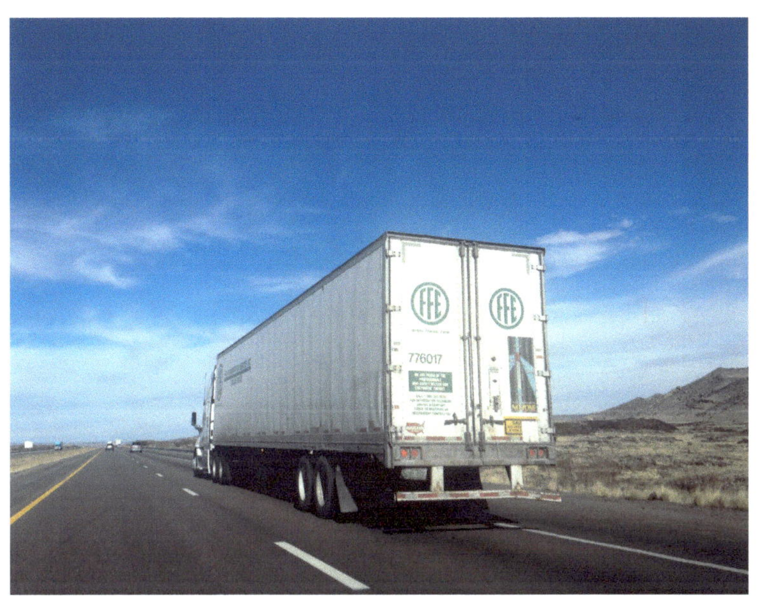
FFE
FFE
776017

I have been to the battlefield at Vicksburg: 4,000 dead in that mud and nearly 30,000 starved and surrendered.

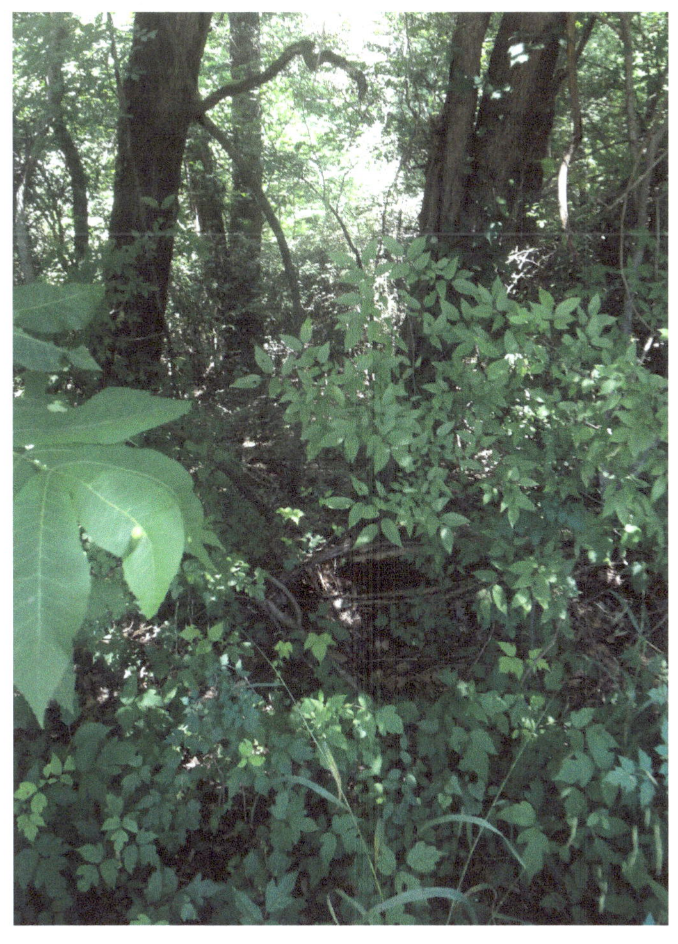

Blood Bank is snow across a desert plain, a worldwide smear of blue and white and gray. It is the silence back behind all these things, much more rare and much more beautiful. I was extraordinarily happy then. It is difficult to think about.

Central Reservation is a thing of beauty set at an impossible distance. It is the 110 freeway in Los Angeles at ten or eleven o'clock at night, passing under the 10, spider-like. It is a love obsessive in nature, hopeless but exhilarating.

The Ghost of Tom Joad is a tender place of synchronous regard.
Later it is soft pain and sweetness over solitary highways.

The White Album is a grassy knoll and summer and a long haired boy who would later drown in a lake, stoned, off the side of a canoe. That was also Led Zeppelin; there were multiple summers. He was the boy everyone knows, who died too young; he was wry, clever, full of promise. He was skinny, and funny. This boy sprawled on the grass howling happiness is a warm gun and why don't we do it in the road. This boy at night in the belly of a small moored boat with cigarettes and other boys.

There was a graveyard in southern Tennessee where the cicadas roared in an unremitting dirge for the dead who were long gone already and the trees hung over weeping and dripping. The dead had been dead there for two hundred years or more and everywhere among them were children. I had only meant to turn around. It was set back from the road, amid great estates with white plank fences. The grasses were groping and wet and it was easy there to see how the wet air held history trapped in between the trees, which all told is a very different thing.

Suffer the little children to come unto me and forbid them not for of such is the kingdom of Heaven.

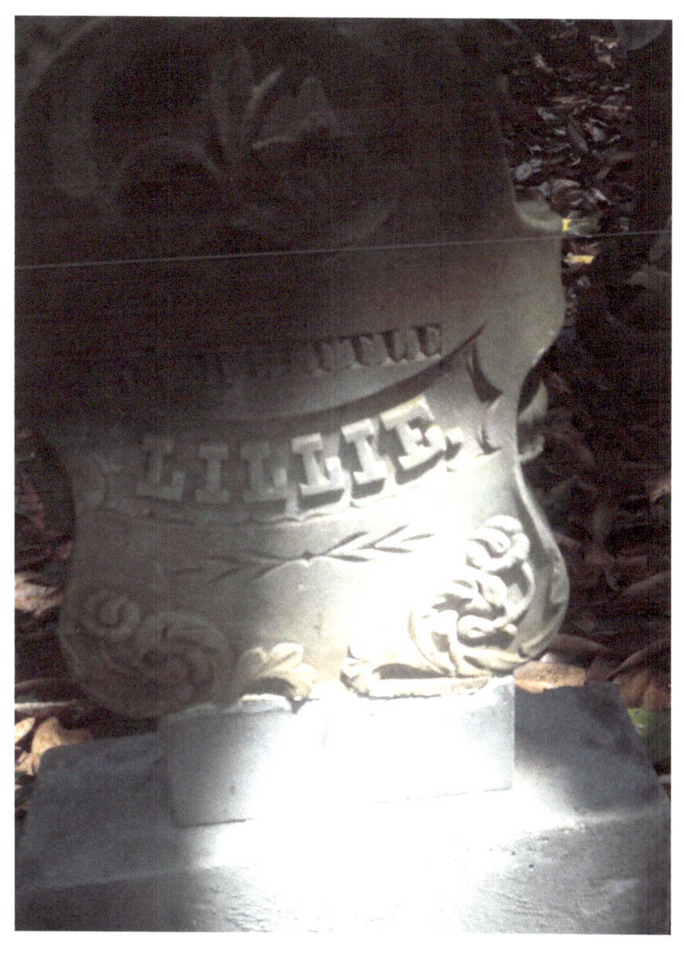
LILLIE.

I have been to the place where Crazy Horse died.

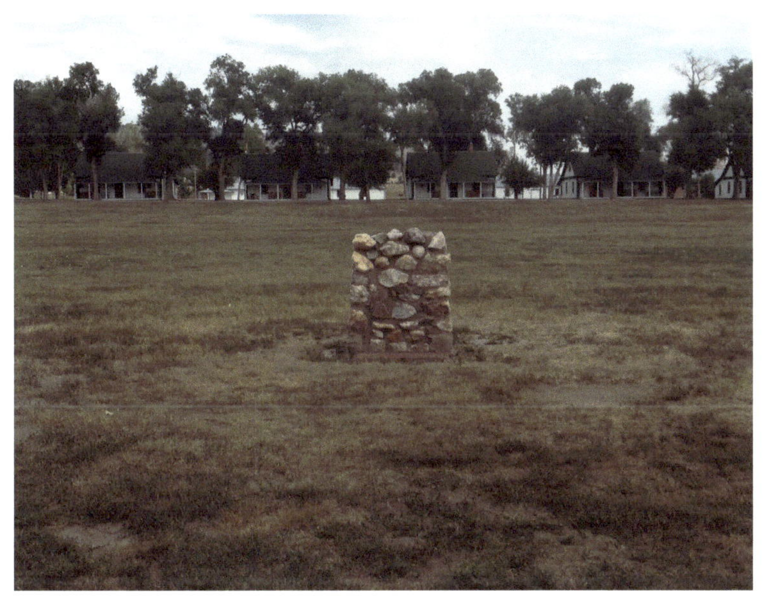

Nothing's Shocking is a pool table in a basement in New Jersey.

Horses is a path out, come to rather late. Its preface is the long stretch of I-40 in January, a clear day, a new year, a great breadth of sky and dread. By May, I was gone. Then the afternoon sun through eucalyptus trees up narrow, winding canyon roads; sometimes a line of traffic all the way up, wealthy commuters and their lawn tenders. I came to understand something about the electric guitar and wondered at having never known.

G-L-O-R-I-A, Gloria ... G-L-O-R-I-A, Gloria ...

I have been to the room where Melville wrote *Moby Dick*. But this was some time ago, I don't have a picture.

I remember a quiet full bookshelf and a worn rug. A gin and tonic in a Sunset Boulevard bar. But these are too much; they would fade in the light. I think of childhood and yes it's real enough but dry, and then I think of the great silent places, for example driving across the Mojave Desert. For example, driving across Nevada. I was thinking about Schopenhauer. You could stop on the road and there was no one. You could stand in the middle of the knowing road. The road was long and straight, over rocky dry hills.

A quiet bookshelf and a worn rug. It is Sketches of Spain. It is Wish Bone. An armchair in the corner, magazines and papers. A window looking out to the wall of another building and to concrete and yet—light. Morning light, early afternoon. Scotch in juice glasses. There was a record player next to the tall bookshelf and light. It is what I remember, the glare of sunlight across cream colored linens. Books. A heavy wood desk and all the places, all the seats and corners. There were three rooms. Light on the desk. Sitting on the floor beside the bookshelf. I remember the table in the kitchen and a window—light—and once in the cabinet there was a little ceramic bird.

I saw the skin of a snake trailing down into a hole. Teddy Roosevelt was here. It is named for him.

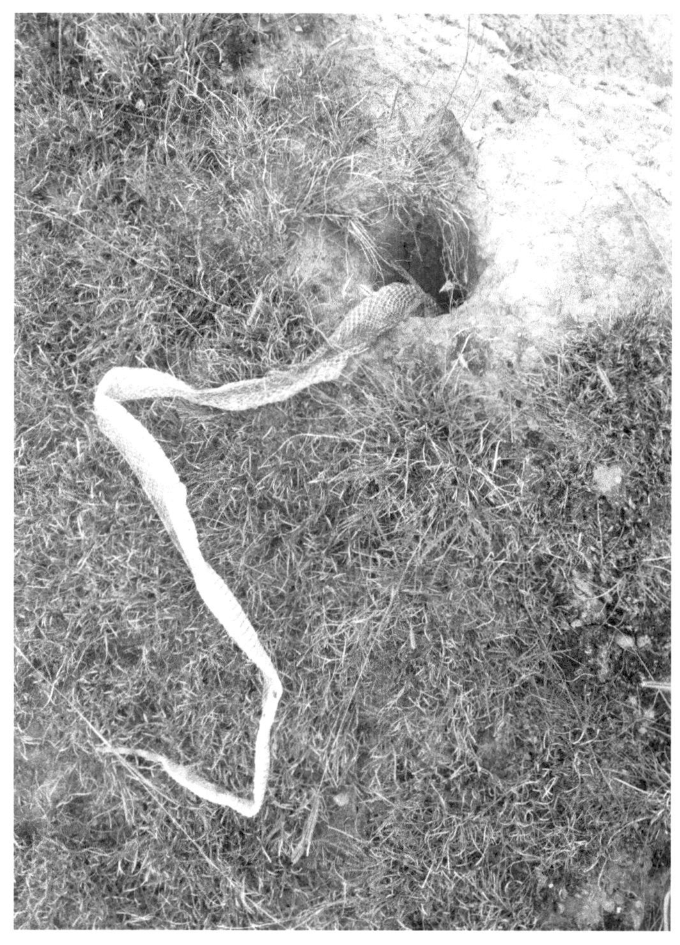

Just Like Honey is the last few moments up a hill with dread, holding to the last of what's mine and will one day see its way out of this.

Abattoir Blues is a farm road with tornadoes at the hem.

I have been to many places where nothing happened in particular.

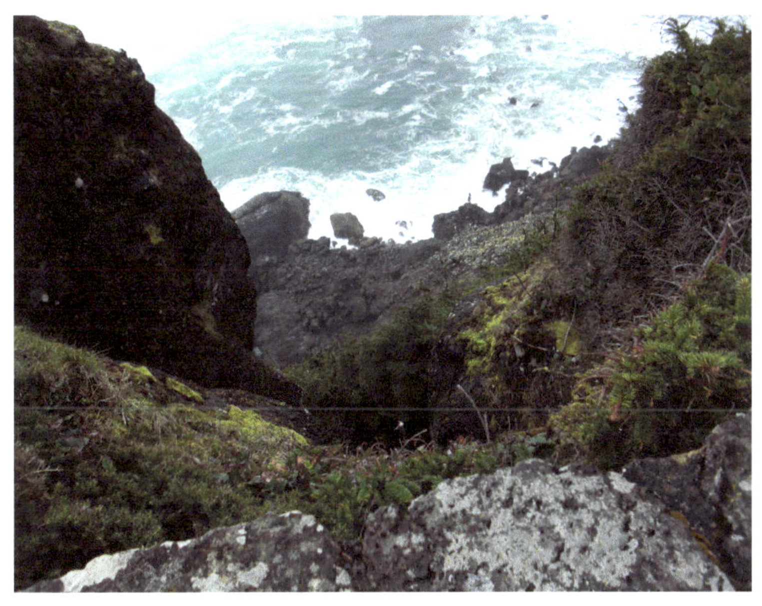

And places where something happened but I don't know what.

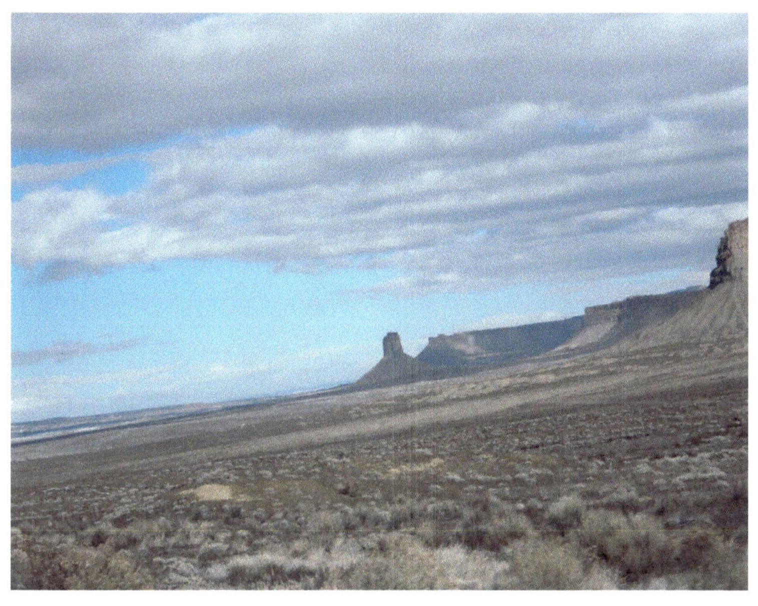

www.ingramcontent.com/pod-product-compliance
Lightning Source LLC
LaVergne TN
LVHW052305100826
845147LV00006B/680

* 9 7 8 1 9 4 7 3 2 2 9 2 9 *